the crystal zodiac

use birthstones to enhance your life

JUDY HALL

bestselling author of *The Crystal Bible*

 A GODSFIELD BOOK

First published in Great Britain in 2004 by Godsfield Press,
a division of Octopus Publishing Group Ltd
2–4 Heron Quays
Docklands
London E14 4JP

Distributed in the United States and Canada by
Sterling Publishing Co., Inc.
387 Park Avenue South, New York, NY 10016-8810

10 9 8 7 6 5 4 3 2 1

Printed and bound in China

ISBN 1 84181 241 2

EAN 9781841812410

The Publishers would like to thanks Holts, gemstone and
jewellery specialists since 1948, for the kind loan of some of
their stones for photography for this book. For further
information visit www.rholt.co.uk.

Disclaimer
The contents of this book do not constitute medical advice,
nor are they intended to take the place of a doctor, and the
services of a qualified crystal healer should be sought for
all medical conditions.

contents

4 introduction

8 crystals and your sun sign

Sun in Aries 10

Sun in Taurus 14

Sun in Gemini 18

Sun in Cancer 22

Sun in Leo 26

Sun in Virgo 30

Sun in Libra 34

Sun in Scorpio 38

Sun in Sagittarius 42

Sun in Capricorn 46

Sun in Aquarius 50

Sun in Pisces 54

58 crystal masks

Aries Ascendant 60

Taurus Ascendant 62

Gemini Ascendant 64

Cancer Ascendant 66

Leo Ascendant 68

Virgo Ascendant 70

Libra Ascendant 72

Scorpio Ascendant 74

Sagittarius Ascendant 76

Capricorn Ascendant 78

Aquarius Ascendant 80

Pisces Ascendant 82

84 how your lunar crystals can help you

Moon in Aries 86

Moon in Taurus 90

Moon in Gemini 94

Moon in Cancer 98

Moon in Leo 102

Moon in Virgo 106

Moon in Libra 110

Moon in Scorpio 114

Moon in Sagittarius 118

Moon in Capricorn 122

Moon in Aquarius 126

Moon in Pisces 130

134 the crystal zodiac mandala

Appendix 138

Index 142

Acknowledgements 144

INTRODUCTION

BIRTHSTONES ARE TRADITIONALLY USED FOR LUCK, ABUNDANCE, PROTECTION AND WISDOM. YOU MAY ALREADY KNOW YOUR BIRTHSTONE BUT NOT EVERYONE AGREES ON WHICH BIRTHSTONE CONNECTS TO WHICH ZODIAC SIGN AND, RATHER THAN THERE BEING ONE BIRTHSTONE FOR EACH SIGN, THERE ARE SEVERAL. THIS BOOK WILL HELP YOU TO SELECT EXACTLY THE RIGHT CRYSTALS FOR YOUR NEEDS. WHATEVER YOU ARE LOOKING FOR, YOUR BIRTHSTONES WILL HARNESS CRYSTAL POWER TO ENHANCE YOUR LIFE.

Each Sun sign is on its own unique journey of self-discovery, a journey that can be accelerated by crystals. Crystals attract beneficial energies, expand your innate potential, balance out less desirable tendencies, overcome your karmic inheritance and connect you to your soul's pathway. Your birth sign is linked to a specific part of the body, giving you a tendency towards ailments of that part. Using appropriate crystals can help these conditions.

Traditionally, crystals were linked to specific signs because the energy of the stone resonated with that sign or with the month in which it fell, or because the planet that ruled the sign or month also governed the crystal. Lusty Mars, for instance, whose colour is red, rules fiery Aries. Both Mars and red are linked to Aries' birthstone, the passionate Ruby. Mars is also one of Scorpio's co-rulers, and Ruby is a companion crystal for this sexy sign.

Such correspondences differ, though, because the links between stars and crystals were determined in the distant past by different sources. Birthstones may come from Western or Eastern cosmology, from esoteric or exoteric traditions. The birthstones and companion crystals in this book have been chosen on the basis of astrological association, compatibility and the life-enhancing qualities the crystals offer. For some signs, two birthstones are listed. In these cases, the two crystals balance and harmonize each other, each offering a much-needed quality.

signs and **ascendants**

Your Sun sign shows you the soul pathway that you are following, but it is only one part of your birthchart. The subtle layering of your personality comes from other factors. Of these, the most easily identified are the Moon and the Ascendant. The combination of Sun, Moon and Ascendant is what makes you uniquely *you*. The Moon represents your emotions and your instinctual approach to life. It shows how you nurture yourself and the expectations, or 'old tapes', that unconsciously run your life. The Ascendant is the face you present to the world, or the mask you put on to conceal your true self. Thanks to the Ascendant effect, people often perceive you differently to how you really are. If your Sun sign does not appear to 'fit', your Moon or Ascendant predominate. (If you don't know your Moon or Ascendant, turn to the Appendix, pages 138–141, to find out.)

In the pages for your Sun sign, you will find your birthstone, companion crystals and your abundance stone. A description of your birthstone, and what it offers you, is followed by the crystals for your potential, challenges, emotions, way of thinking, soul pathway and healing. Finally, there is a special crystal birthday ritual to energize your wishes for the coming year.

Crystal Masks tells you your Ascendant crystal, and what other crystals you can use to offset or enhance your Sun-sign characteristics, with an Ascendant oriented meditation you can do whenever you feel the need.

In each Moon sign section, you will find your Moon and lunar crystals, and crystals that enhance your intuition, together with a ritual for attracting love, forgiveness, truth, and so on. These rituals can, of course, be carried out by anyone who will find them beneficial, and are listed in the index.

Everyone has something of all 12 zodiac signs within them, which is why the book ends with an astrological mandala. Making the mandala brings you into harmony with the whole and aligns you with the astrological maxim: *As above, so below. As without, so within.*

using your **zodiac crystals**

Crystals take many forms. Some of the birthstones in this book are precious gemstones – Diamond and Sapphire, for example – but there are semi-precious stones, such as Peridot or Topaz; and others are opaque, such as Onyx. Gemstones tend to be the prettiest and most expensive, and opaque stones the cheapest and, superficially, less attractive – but all crystal forms have their own unique properties that are unrelated to cost or appearance, and non-gem quality stones have the same attributes as the more expensive, faceted gem form.

All gemstones can be obtained as clear, faceted stones or uncut, non-gem quality stones. While the faceted stones look stunning, the uncut opaque form, which is available as a smooth and shiny tumbled piece, is equally powerful. Tumbled non-gem stones are extremely robust and ideal for healing layouts or mandalas. If you wish to use faceted gemstones, these should be set as rings, necklaces, bracelets or earrings to protect them and to keep them in contact with your skin. You may wish to substitute less expensive crystals for gemstones (see the chart opposite), especially where these are to be used for mandalas, crystal healing or meditations.

Tumbled stones can be stored together in a bag, but delicate crystals should be separately wrapped and kept in a box when not in use to avoid scratching.

Buying crystals need not be expensive. The best place to buy uncut or tumbled stones is at a crystal shop, while rarer pieces are available through the internet. Handling crystals allows 'your' crystal to be attracted to you. If you plunge your hand into a tub of crystals, the right one sticks to your fingers. Or if one catches your eye as you enter the store, that is the crystal for you. Remember that biggest is not necessarily best, nor is the most beautiful the most powerful.

Your crystal needs to be cleansed and dedicated before use. The simplest way to cleanse negative vibes from a crystal is to hold it under running water for a few moments and then place it in the Sun to re-energize. Porous or friable crystals, however, may be damaged by water. These are best placed in rice or on a Carnelian. When the crystal is cleansed and re-energized, hold it in your hands for a few moments and dedicate it to your highest good. Picture it surrounded by light, then clearly state your intention for the crystal, to programme it.

To gain maximum benefit from your crystal, wear it constantly, preferably touching your skin, and cleanse it regularly. Carrying your abundance stone, or placing it in the far left corner of a room, attracts wealth and good fortune and is an excellent starting point for introducing the power of crystals into your life. Putting your favourite crystal under your pillow at night, or meditating with it, is enormously helpful. For healing, hold the crystal over the affected site for 15 to 20 minutes daily. If other people handle your crystals, or you use them for healing, remember to cleanse them afterwards.

gemstone   suitable substitute

RUBY   GARNET

DIAMOND   CLEAR QUARTZ

EMERALD   PERIDOT

SAPPHIRE   LAPIS LAZULI

CRYSTALS AND
YOUR SUN SIGN

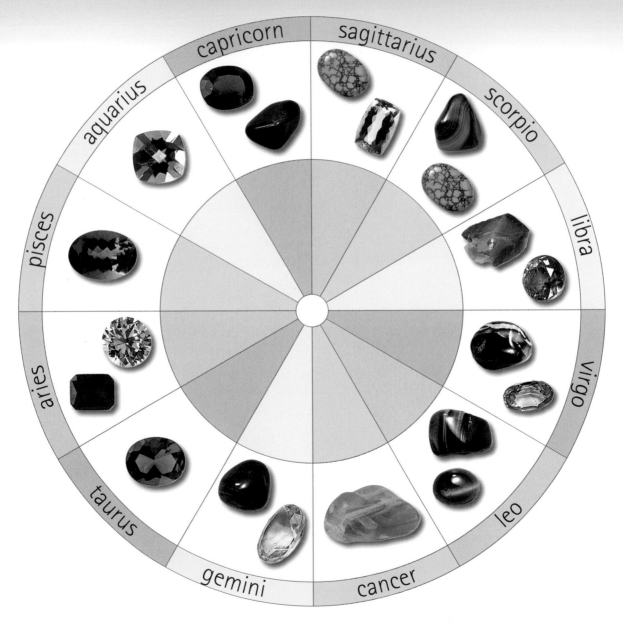

Ancient man looked at the sky and perceived the band of the constellations, against which the Sun travelled, as a mythical story. The most prominent constellations, which divided the pathway into 12 roughly equal divisions, became the 12 Sun-signs that we know today as the zodiac, and the symbols became glyphs for the signs. Aries, for instance, was seen as a giant ram and the ram's horns became headstrong Aries' glyph. Scorpio, whose emblem is the scorpion and who has a barbed tongue, has a glyph with a sting in its tail.

These zodiac signs were linked to 12 personality types, each of whom shared certain traits. Each sign has its own unique colour and qualities, drives and challenges, needs and desires. Each has a distinctive personality and a particular way of looking at the world. As the Sun traverses the zodiac, it takes on the colour of the individual signs.

Crystals too have taken on celestial energy; the Sun has irradiated them for millions of years, so there is a natural affinity between crystals and the Sun. Crystals are characterized by a unique 'lattice' formation within the crystal which, as science has shown, is capable of absorbing and retaining energy. When you wear your birthstone, this energy is released, which is why birthstones are powerful tools for self-transformation and healing. The most effective way of harnessing this power is to hold or wear your crystal. This transfers the crystal vibrations into your subtle energy field and your physical body.

sun in aries
the ram
MARCH 21–APRIL 19

BIRTHSTONES Ruby, Diamond

ABUNDANCE STONE Carnelian

RITUAL CRYSTAL Fire Agate

COMPANION CRYSTALS Amethyst, Aquamarine, Aventurine, Bloodstone (Heliotrope), Carnelian, Citrine, Fire Agate, Garnet, Iron Pyrite, Jadeite, Jasper, Kunzite, Magnetite, Pink Tourmaline, Orange Spinel, Spinel, Topaz

your aries **birthstones** and you

RUBY

DIAMOND

Your birthstones are the fiery Ruby and the ice cool Diamond. Your vigorous nature is reflected in the scintillating red of a faceted Ruby and the smouldering incandescence of the tumbled stone. This crystal resonates with your passion and vitality. It aligns your ideals and your will, enabling you to focus on the task ahead and supports the dynamic leadership that comes so naturally to you.

Ruby spices up your life, but this is not always to your advantage. Ruby can be exciting, yes, but it can also over-stimulate. You do not suffer fools gladly and Ruby draws anger to the surface for dissipation but, in the process, may overheat situations, bringing you into the danger on which you thrive. (Carrying a Carnelian helps protect you when in the danger zone.) Ruby may also make you more self-centred and self-absorbed, the less desirable side of Aries. The calming influence of your other birthstone, Diamond, offsets this by bringing you the gifts of thoughtfulness and consideration for others. Diamond also helps you to bond with your partner, overcoming a tendency to put yourself first in all things. This scintillating stone helps you to make your life a cohesive whole and reminds you of your soul's purpose.

crystals and your **potential**

You were born with the ability to assert yourself, along with abundant courage and stamina. People follow your lead, but may not like where you leave them. Persistence is not your strong point, which means many projects are started, but few completed. Aventurine assists you in harnessing your leadership qualities to perseverance. It ameliorates anger and gently diffuses explosive situations. Wearing this stone maximizes your potential for strong leadership and decisive action; it helps you to right wrongs and to fight for a good cause.

IRON PYRITE

If you are a woman, combining Aventurine with Iron Pyrite, a stone closely associated with your ruler, Mars, adds tenacity to the task and brings you the gift of diplomacy. Iron Pyrite, however, may be too 'macho' for some men, propelling them into over-confidence and aggression. The beautiful pink-enfolded-within-green of Watermelon Tourmaline brings tact and the ability to understand the inner workings of situations.

WATERMELON TOURMALINE

crystals and your **challenges**

As an Aries, your greatest challenge in life is to think before you act. Jasper promotes thought before action and helps you to understand the consequences of your behaviour. Aries can be a headstrong, abrasive sign, given to rudeness and impatience. Howlite calms your personality and brings peace to your surroundings, helping you to work in co-operation with others. You dislike criticism, even when this could be helpful, and Citrine encourages the acceptance of constructive criticism, and shows you how to act on it. It also assists you to be spontaneous without trampling on other people in the process.

RED JASPER

Despite the impulsiveness of your nature, procrastination can be a problem. This often reflects ambivalence around a course of action that someone else is insisting on, but it can also reflect your innate dislike of 'doing the wrong thing'. Any hesitancy is quickly overcome by your fiery Ruby birthstone, and wearing a Diamond heightens your innate fearlessness in rising to a challenge.

CITRINE

crystals and your **emotions**

Aries do not have much time for emotion, and other signs accuse you of being insensitive. Nevertheless, you have volatile emotions. Many of these centre around lust and love – and your dislike of injustice. A libido as strong as yours demands to be acted upon, and yet you have a surprisingly romantic streak. Pink Tourmaline is an ideal stone for you. This beautiful stone encourages love at all levels, gently disperses emotional pain and dissolves destructive feelings. An excellent heart protector, it is an aphrodisiac – although Aries rarely needs this. It teaches you that it is safe to love, instilling a confidence that Aries sometimes lacks, and introduces the qualities of compassion and wisdom into your dealings with others.

crystals and your **way of thinking**

You tend to think in terms of black and white, things either are, or are not. Strongly opinionated, your most used words are 'I think you'll find I'm right', and it is exceedingly difficult to persuade you otherwise. Aragonite is an excellent stone for promoting mental flexibility and the ability to see the bigger picture. It helps you to 'think outside the box'.

crystals and your **soul pathway**

Aries is on a soul pathway of developing the self, unselfishly. You are becoming centred within your Self, the highest part of your being, rather than in your ego, the personality-based small self. Connecting to your Self is strengthened by meditating with an iridescent Aqua Aura crystal, which harnesses your abundant life energy to a soul connection that reaches to the highest vibrations. Tranquil and delicate, Kunzite helps you to open your heart to unconditional love and peace and shows you how to project this gentle, uplifting vibration into all your relationships. Worn over the heart, this stone brings humility, promoting tolerance of others and unselfish love of one's Self.

aries **crystal healing**

Aries is associated with the head, and your sign suffers from headaches, neuralgia and the like. Placing an Amethyst crystal on your forehead for 15 to 20 minutes soothes the pain and induces relaxation in your body. Being a restless, highly active sign, you are prone to stress and associated disorders such as insomnia. Taking the time to lie flat with a Clear Quartz placed point-down above your head, an Amethyst point on your forehead, a piece of Kunzite over your heart, a Citrine over your solar plexus and a Smoky Quartz placed point-down below your feet, draws off stress and negativity from your body and brings in quiet, refreshing peace.

AMETHYST

The adrenal and suprarenal glands are also connected to Aries. These glands produce adrenaline and overproduction of adrenaline, the result of stress, keeps the body wired. They can be calmed by placing two Green Calcite crystals on your back, about a handspan above your waist and to each side of your spine.

SMOKY QUARTZ

Luminescent Fire Agate is an excellent all-round healing stone for Aries and can be worn for long periods of time. It has a strong grounding ability, which supports your body, and protects against ill-wishing – especially useful as your forthright speech tends to, inadvertently, upset those around you. Fire Agate is a 'mellowing out' stone and can be used as a meditation aid. This crystal balances the endocrine system and keeps the heat processes within the body stable. It also prevents burnout and exhaustion.

GREEN CALCITE

aries **birthday ritual**

On your birthday, sit quietly holding your Fire Agate, bringing your attention deep into your self. Pass your crystal over the flame of a candle to cleanse and purify it. Holding your crystal in your lap, picture a sacred flame spreading out from the crystal to enfold your whole body. This sacred flame forms a cloak of protection around you, replenishing your vitality and giving you a calm centre. Its powerful energy ignites your creativity. Now picture whatever you wish for yourself flowing out across the next year of your life. When you are ready, bring your attention back into the room.

FIRE AGATE

sun in taurus
the bull
APRIL 20—MAY 20

your taurus **birthstone** and you

EMERALD

PERIDOT

Your planetary ruler is the voluptuous Venus, the goddess of love, and your Emerald birthstone is her favourite stone – so it is no surprise that outwardly you are a sensible and pragmatic soul but inwardly you are sensual and hedonistic. Like Venus, you relish all the good things of life, valuing your comfort, and Emerald encourages you to enjoy life to the full. This is a life-affirming stone with great integrity.

Emerald is known as 'the stone of successful love' and wearing an Emerald helps you to find the loyal and steadfast love you associate with domestic bliss, and it also attracts a loving outlet for your sensuality. Emerald enhances your strength of character, and enables you to overcome the misfortunes of life. You dislike change and your birthstone promotes enduring partnership. An Emerald is said to protect against enchantments and to change colour where there is unfaithfulness. You appreciate this warning as you find it difficult to forgive – or forget. Fortunately, Emerald helps you to heal negative feelings and supports your infinite patience.

crystals and your **potential**

Taurus has a strong connection with the earth. You take matter, shape it and create with it, working in an extremely practical way. Creating a healthy, pollution-free environment is one of Taurus' soul wishes and you are supported in this by many of your companion crystals, but Aragonite is a particularly reliable earth healer.

ARAGONITE

If you are dedicated to reaching your highest potential, then Malachite can assist. This stone is powerfully transformative and requires strength and endurance when working, qualities you have in abundance. It encourages risk taking and change. Mercilessly showing what is blocking your growth, it breaks outgrown ties and outworn patterns. Teaching how to take responsibility for your own life, Malachite releases your inhibitions and pushes you onwards.

MALACHITE

crystals and your **challenges**

The infinite patience of Emerald resonates with your own nature but there are times when this patient approach to life becomes a handicap. Your sign is noted for holding on to the status quo and Peridot is the stone *par excellence* for facilitating necessary change. Taurus can be extremely fixed and you are the archetypal square peg in a round hole who tries to accommodate the discomfort rather than find a place which fits your abilities. Aquamarine offers you the courage to climb out of the hole.

AQUAMARINE

The intense midnight blue of Lapis Lazuli encourages you to raise your eyes to the heavens, opening your intuitive side and taking you beyond the material world. This opening of the intuition is also facilitated by translucent Selenite, which creates a feeling of safety while encouraging you to reach out to the spiritual realm.

SELENITE

crystals and your **emotions**

Taurus has powerful emotions that can be deeply entrenched. Your most destructive emotions are resentment, jealousy and possessiveness. Resentment dissolves under the influence of Rhodonite (see the Forgiveness ritual, page 117), and this stone also

RHODONITE

TOPAZ

GREEN TOURMALINE

BLUE CHALCEDONY

assists forgiveness and fosters reconciliation. An emotional balancer that nurtures love and heals emotional scars, Rhodonite assists in bringing back into yourself any emotions that have been projected on to a partner.

Your possessiveness arises out of your desire to hold on to what you feel is yours, be it a person or a possession, and out of your deep-seated fear of change. Topaz helps you to let go gracefully, trusting that what is meant to be will be. Nothing negative survives around joyful, vibrant Topaz, so it is an excellent stone for lightening dark emotions.

Jealousy is ameliorated by one of the most useful stones for Taurus, Peridot. This stone also clears resentment and imparts confidence in yourself. It banishes lethargy and helps you to admit to any mistakes you have made, enabling you to move on into a positive future.

crystals and your **way of thinking**

Your thought processes are practical, slow and deliberate, and yet creative. Taurus has a rigid way of thinking with dogmatic opinions and, as a result, it is difficult for you to envisage new possibilities. Tourmaline promotes flexibility of thought and Green Tourmaline is particularly appropriate as it enables you to see all possible solutions and to select the one which is most constructive. Botswana Agate is also beneficial in that it opens up the bigger picture. This stone helps you to explore unknown territory and access your creativity. If you are afraid to express your thoughts for fear of being judged, then Blue Lace Agate gently dissolves your fears and facilitates clear communication, promoting compassionate listening in those to whom you express yourself. Both Malachite and Aquamarine help you to put yourself in someone else's place and see the world from their perspective. These stones ameliorate intolerance and overcome conflict and contradictions.

Taurus often speaks slowly, reflecting the deliberation that goes on before you open your mouth. Blue Chalcedony not only enlarges your mind to assimilate new ideas and accept new situations, it also speeds up your intellectual processes, and improves your mental and verbal dexterity.

crystals and your **soul pathway**

With your Sun in Taurus, your soul is on a pathway that seeks inner security rather than external safety. Rutilated Quartz, sometimes known as Angel Hair, is renowned for its ability to illuminate the spiritual pathway. Keeping a piece of Rutilated Quartz with you at all times serves as a reminder of the presence of your spiritual self and brings about deep insights into what is preventing you from trusting the universe. Once this trust is established, you have inner security, one of the few qualities that can be taken out of this world.

RUTILATED QUARTZ

taurus **crystal healing**

Taurus is connected with the neck and shoulders and health problems centre around the throat and the thyroid. Blue Lace Agate is an excellent throat healer as it removes the blocks to self-expression that can underlie dis-eases of the throat and stiffness in the neck and shoulders. Blue Lace Agate can be made into a gargle by immersing the stone in spring water and placing it in sunlight for a few hours. The water should be sipped or gargled several times a day. Blue Lace Agate is particularly beneficial for thyroid deficiencies and should be worn continuously at the throat to stimulate the thyroid and to assist self-expression. Lapis Lazuli is another powerful healing stone for the thyroid or larynx that alleviates painful throat conditions.

BLUE LACE AGATE

LAPIS LAZULI

taurus **birthday ritual**

Sit quietly holding a pair of Boji Stones, bringing your attention deep into your self. Touch the stones to the ground to cleanse them. Holding your stones, picture a cord connecting them deep into the earth. Feel energy rising up this cord to form a cloak of protection around your whole body, washing away your fears and giving you a calm centre. Its powerful energy ignites your creativity. Now picture whatever you wish for yourself flowing out across the next year. When you are ready, bring your attention back into the room and place your stones where you will see them often.

BOJI STONES

sun in gemini
the twins
MAY 21–JUNE 20

BIRTHSTONES Agate, Tourmaline

ABUNDANCE STONE Dendritic Agate

RITUAL CRYSTAL Apophyllite

COMPANION CRYSTALS Apatite, Apophyllite, Aquamarine, Blue Spinel, Calcite, Chrysocolla, Chrysoprase, Citrine, Dendritic Agate, Dendritic Chalcedony, Green Obsidian, Green Tourmaline, Hiddenite (Green Kunzite), Howlite, Rutilated Quartz (Angel Hair), Sapphire, Serpentine, Sugilite, Tourmalinated Quartz, Tiger's Eye, Topaz, Variscite

your gemini **birthstones** and you

BLUE AGATE

BLUE TOURMALINE

Gemini is extremely active, both physically and mentally. Your innate ability to multi-task is strengthened by your Agate birthstone since this stable and grounding stone encourages you to pay precise attention to details while still seeing the bigger picture. This stone's multiple layers bring hidden information to light. Agate is also invaluable in avoiding the nervous tension to which you are prone. Gemini is what is known as a dual sign, that is, it has two sides to its nature, and Agate has the ability to integrate this duality.

However, Agate works slowly, which can trigger your natural impatience. Your other birthstone, Tourmaline, works faster and is equally appropriate for a dual sign as it balances the two sides of the brain, and integrates your inner and outer selves. It draws off negative energies and stabilizes your tendency to fly off in too many directions at once. Brown Tourmaline is particularly useful as it grounds you and assists in paying attention to practical matters.

crystals and your **potential**

Communication is, without doubt, Gemini's forte. You have the ability to gather in an enormous amount of information from disparate sources and to distil the essence so that it can be passed on to others. You make intuitive connections and assumptions that are inspired. In your excitement, however, you rush into sharing your perceptions, and often speak without thinking of the consequences. Chrysocolla is useful for you because it teaches when to keep silent and when to speak. Your weighty Agate birthstone adds depth to your communication, which may otherwise be at a rather superficial level.

crystals and your **challenges**

One of Gemini's major challenges is in identifying what exactly is truth. You have the ability to argue that black is black, that black is white, and that it is black again, without even noticing that you have switched views. Gemini can also be very creative with the truth – especially when concocting little white lies – and your birthstone, Agate, helps to promote veracity. Your affinity with the Stone of Truth, Apophyllite, overcomes your tendency to disregard inconvenient facts. Dendritic Chalcedony assists you in facing up to unpleasant facts that you would otherwise gloss over, and Blue Topaz helps you to recognize where you have strayed from your own truth and returns you to its core. With such a strong emphasis on the mental side of your make-up, it is helpful to sit quietly with a Serpentine crystal and allow it to gently ground you into the physical realm, while at the same time letting it open up the channels for spiritual communication.

crystals and your **emotions**

Gemini loves talking about feelings, but actually feeling them is another matter. Your emotions are superficial and talking is used to hide feelings. Howlite encourages emotional expression and Variscite helps you to reveal yourself to the world as you are.

crystals and your **way of thinking**

The Gemini mind is versatile, curious, over-active and quick-witted. Your challenge is to avoid mental stress and Aquamarine is beneficial in calming your mind and removing extraneous thoughts. It filters the information reaching your brain and clarifies your mental processes. Calcite assists in practising discernment, especially knowing which information is important and which can be disregarded. It also links your mind to your emotions, facilitating emotional intelligence. In its green form, Calcite is a powerful mental healer that restores balance to the mind. It stabilizes your butterfly mind, enabling you to concentrate on one thing at a time instead of paying minimal attention to a myriad thoughts. Howlite also calms the mind, assisting sleep or meditation, and allowing reasoned communication to take place at times of intense pressure. Chrysanthemum Stone counteracts superficiality of thought and guards against distractions. Keep one on your desk as you work.

crystals and your **soul pathway**

You are on a pathway of clear and unambiguous communication of who you are. Your soul needs you to recognize that there are many levels to the universe. The communication has to be not only at the physical and mental levels, but also at the emotional and spiritual levels. Apophyllite is an excellent crystal for facilitating your pathway. It creates a conscious connection between the physical and spiritual worlds, and opens a dialogue between the two. Sources of the highest spiritual guidance can be accessed by holding a Rutilated Quartz (Angel Hair).

gemini **crystal healing**

As you rarely stop to rest, you are prone to nervous exhaustion. This can be alleviated by Golden (Imperial) Topaz, which acts like a battery and recharges your energy. Lying for 15 minutes – longer if possible – and holding a Topaz is extremely beneficial. Topaz can also be worn for long periods of time.

Gemini is associated with the respiratory system, the hands and arms, and the thymus gland that governs the immune system. Hiddenite, the green form of Kunzite, is a great healer for the thymus and the lungs. It should be placed or worn just above the heart, where the thymus gland is located. Taping one in place and leaving overnight is a quick-acting immune stimulator, as is Green Tourmaline. For an acute infection, tape a Bloodstone (Heliotrope) over your thymus. An elixir made by placing any of these crystals in a glass of spring water, which is then stood in the Sun for several hours, is beneficial if sipped at intervals throughout the day. Place these crystals around your bed at night to enhance your immune system.

HIDDENITE

Apophyllite is an efficient healer for respiratory ailments, especially asthma. If an Apophyllite crystal or cluster is held to the chest during an attack it is swiftly ameliorated. Chrysocolla also benefits the respiratory system. It re-oxygenates the blood and improves the cellular structure of the lungs, increasing the breathing capacity, and this crystal can be placed under the pillow at night.

BLOODSTONE

People with the Sun in Gemini are often sensitive to weather changes and environmental pollutants, which create conditions such as seasonal affective disorder or eczema. Moss Agate, either worn or placed on the body, alleviates these conditions. With such a busy mind, Gemini often suffers from insomnia. Howlite soothes and quietens the mind, shutting off extraneous thoughts. Pop one under your pillow for sweet dreams and a good night's sleep.

MOSS AGATE

gemini **birthday ritual**

Sit quietly holding your Apophyllite, bringing your attention deep into your self. Blow gently on the crystal to cleanse it. Holding your Apophyllite above your head, picture a pyramid of light forming from the crystal down to, and under, your feet. Feel celestial energy flowing down into the pyramid to form a cloak of protection around your whole body, dissolving your worries, and giving you a calm centre. Its powerful energy ignites your creativity. Now picture whatever you wish for yourself flowing out across the next year of your life. When you are ready, bring your attention back into the room and place your Apophyllite where you will see it often.

APOPHYLLITE

sun in cancer
the crab
JUNE 21—JULY 22

BIRTHSTONE Moonstone

ABUNDANCE STONE Moonstone

RITUAL STONE Calcite

COMPANION CRYSTALS Amber,

Beryl, Brown Spinel, Calcite, Carnelian,

Chalcedony, Chrysoprase, Emerald,

Howlite, Jasper, Opal, Petalite, Pink

Tourmaline, Rhodonite, Ruby

your cancer **birthstone** and you

MOONSTONE

Your birthstone, Moonstone, is a 'stone of new beginnings' and is strongly connected to the Moon and to intuition. As a Moon-ruled sign, you are naturally intuitive and Moonstone assists you to harness that intuition and apply it practically. Worn as a pendant, Moonstone not only enhances your psychic gifts but also encourages acceptance of them. Worn as earrings, or placed on the forehead, Moonstone assists in developing clairvoyance and clairaudience. Moonstone encourages lucid dreaming, and makes the unconscious conscious. However, care must be taken that Moonstone does not encourage illusions based on wishful thinking.

Moonstone's effect is particularly strong at the full Moon, so at this time you may need to remove it unless you are in a space where meditation and inward reflection can occur.

With your Sun in Cancer you are highly sensitive and prone to mood swings, but Moonstone can keep you emotionally balanced. This stone reminds you that everything is part of a fluctuating cycle, and assists in understanding your emotions, ameliorating inner feelings of vulnerability. Linking with the biorhythmic clock that governs your body and your moods, holding Moonstone attunes you to your own unique biorhythm cycle.

crystals and your **potential**

Compassionate and caring, Cancer has enormous potential for nurturing. Chalcedony is a prime nurturing stone that promotes brotherhood and group stability. If you keep this stone with you, your own energies will not become exhausted. Chalcedony also teaches you how to care about, rather than for, others. It allows you to do what is necessary, and then to encourage the other person to stand on their own feet.

Yours is a highly ambitious sign, although you hide it well. The passion and energy of Ruby propel you forward into realizing your ambitions and will attract an outlet for your hidden talents

crystals and your **challenges**

As one of the signs that values routine and hesitates to make changes, you may find that your life has become static. Moonstone opens you to the possibility of serendipity and synchronicity. One of your major challenges is that of letting go, especially of people and the past, and this is facilitated by the use of Dendritic Chalcedony, which helps you to face up to unpleasant matters in the past and to process your memories so that you can move on. Pink Tourmaline also facilitates letting go of the past and prevents emotional overload. Fire Agate is a useful aid in promoting the inner security that is the antidote to your emotional vulnerability. Cutting the apron strings is extremely beneficial for you as otherwise you can smother or drive away those you love (see the Tie cutting ritual, page 101).

crystals and your **emotions**

Your sign is one of the most emotional in the zodiac and your Moonstone birthstone is conducive to emotional stability. It prevents over-reaction to an emotional stimulus and encourages emotional intelligence. Placed on the solar plexus, it draws out emotional patterns that no longer serve you and provides deep emotional healing.

CHRYSOPRASE

Rhodonite has the ability to clear away emotional scars from the past. Chrysoprase heals the emotional dependence, or co-dependence, to which you are prone. It supports independence without losing commitment. If you need help cutting the ties with anyone from your past, Sunstone and Petalite assist with this. Preventing worry, Beryl teaches you to do only that which needs doing and shows how to shed unnecessary emotional baggage. If things do not go the way you envisage them, Rhodonite assists you in forgiving and forgetting, and encourages taking back emotions that have been projected on to a partner.

SUNSTONE

Home is very important to you as it provides security and stability. With a secure home environment to return to, you venture confidently into the world. Without one, you are emotionally adrift. Chrysocolla is an excellent stone for you. It draws off negative energy within the home and helps you to accept with serenity a changing environment. Chrysocolla also ameliorates your tendency to be extremely touchy, it desensitizes you and imparts confidence.

crystals and your **way of thinking**

PETALITE

Cancer never approaches anything head on, thinking is circuitous, and yet you are deeply perceptive. You may need a Ruby to sharpen your mind and heighten your concentration. Aquamarine is excellent for showing you what is important and what can be ignored. You are able to pick up other people's thoughts and feelings easily, and may confuse them with your own. Opal helps you to differentiate, and amplifies someone else's thoughts before returning them to the sender. It teaches that what you put out, comes back to you. This sensitive stone helps you to tune into undercurrents and higher awareness, bringing both into the light of consciousness.

OPAL

crystals and your **soul pathway**

Your soul pathway centres around dispassionate nurturing and Jasper, known as 'the supreme nurturer', reminds people to help each other. This stone sustains and supports the soul during times of stress, bringing tranquillity and wholeness.

cancer **crystal healing**

Cancer rules the stomach and alimentary canal and you are prone to ulcers, irritable bowel syndrome and indigestion. Such conditions are caused by the effect of emotions such as worry on the body and your birthstone, Moonstone, is excellent for soothing psychosomatic dis-ease of this kind. Keep it about your person and hold it when you need to remain emotionally calm. Rhodonite is useful for healing stomach ulcers and can be drunk as an elixir, made by placing the crystal in spring water and standing it in the Sun for several hours. It is excellent for shock or trauma.

Moonstone is also highly effective in healing disorders or disturbances of the female reproductive system, and for stabilizing the fluid balance in the body, especially in the lymphatic system. It quickly clears fluid retention and alleviates PMS when placed over the uterus. Carnelian can be helpful if fertility is an issue. If you have difficulty in breast feeding a child, place Moonstone or Pink Chalcedony on your breasts for 15 minutes or so before a feed and the milk will be increased. This also soothes inflamed breasts.

cancer **birthday ritual**

On your birthday, place your Calcite under running water to cleanse and purify it. Sit quietly holding your Calcite, bringing your attention deep into your self. Holding your crystal over your solar plexus, picture a bubble of energy radiating out from the crystal to surround your whole body. Feel energy flowing out of the crystal to form a cloak of protection around you. Allow the stone to absorb your negative and outworn emotions, giving you a calm centre. Its powerful energy ignites your creativity and power of manifestation. Now picture whatever you wish for yourself flowing out across the next year of your life. When you are ready, bring your attention back into the room and place your Calcite where you will see it often.

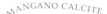

sun in leo
the lion

JULY 23–AUGUST 22

BIRTHSTONE Cat's Eye (or Tiger's Eye)

ABUNDANCE STONE Tiger's Eye

RITUAL CRYSTAL Red Garnet

COMPANION CRYSTALS Amber, Boji Stone, Carnelian, Chrysocolla, Citrine, Danburite, Emerald, Garnet, Golden Beryl, Green Tourmaline, Hiddenite, Kunzite, Larimar, Morganite (Pink Beryl), Muscovite, Onyx, Orange Calcite, Petalite, Pink Tourmaline, Pyrolusite, Quartz, Red Obsidian, Rhodochrosite, Ruby, Topaz, Turquoise

CAT'S EYE

TIGER'S EYE

your Leo **birthstone** and you

Leo has an abundant choice of birthstones, and traditional associations are with yellow stones that reflect the light of your ruler, the Sun. The ostentatiousness of the rare and beautiful Cat's Eye appeals to you, though the beautifully banded Tiger's Eye is an excellent, and cheaper, alternative. Like it, you radiate benevolent warmth – until someone upsets your dignity. Cat's Eye keeps you serene by enhancing your natural confidence and joy. Wear your Cat's Eye (or Tiger's Eye) on the right-hand side of the body for maximum benefit. This stone combines the energy of the earth with the Sun to create a grounded and yet extremely high vibration. The golden form of Tiger's Eye in particular resonates with your sunny self but any Tiger's Eye is protective and facilitates constructive manifestation of your strong will. It helps you to differentiate between what you wish for and what you really need, and supports your innate integrity. Tiger's Eye is an excellent stone for promoting your latent talents and unblocking your creative abilities.

crystals and your **potential**

Leo is known for its vigour and vitality, although, you may need a stimulus to move in a new direction. Sunny Topaz, with its ability to overcome limitations, helps you to gain the recognition you crave. Use it to develop creative potential. Its vibrant energy stimulates your own natural generosity and assists you to be the big-hearted Leo you were made to be. This stone helps you to recognize your own inner riches as well as drawing to you all the support you need.

A natural performer, you want to take a starring role on life's stage and Golden (Imperial) Topaz is the stone for you. Wearing it bestows charisma and confidence, allowing you to take pride in your own achievements without becoming boastful.

TOPAZ

TOPAZ

crystals and your **challenges**

The challenge of using your power wisely is facilitated by Tiger's Eye. It teaches you how to recognize your inner resources and apply these to achieving goals. The power you should be seeking is not power over others, but rather self-empowerment and this is facilitated by Tiger's Eye. Tiger's Eye is also helpful in dealing with another challenge, overcoming your considerable pride. Leo never admits to having faults, but Tiger's Eye combined with gentle Kunzite brings about humility, while Topaz overcomes injured pride and restores your usual sunny self. Wearing Hiddentite helps you to stand in your power rather than being taken over by it.

KUNZITE

crystals and your **emotions**

As a heart-centred sign, Leo has strong emotions, especially around sex and sexuality. You find it hard to hide your emotions and usually express them freely. However, Leo is both proud and fixed, and you have a tendency to hold on to emotional hurts, retreating into wounded dignity. If this occurs, Rhodochrosite or Rose Quartz are powerful emotional healers. Place them over your heart and let them draw out the pain, softening your attitude to the offending person as they do so.

ROSE QUARTZ

RUBY

Leo is closely associated with the heart, and vibrant Ruby is a wonderful stone for stimulating and opening the heart, although some Leo's find its redness too stimulating. Ruby encourages you to 'follow your bliss' but it is also a protector for the heart. With your abundant vitality, you may well attract people who vampirize your heart energy, drawing it off to use themselves. Wearing a Ruby prevents this, while at the same time promoting the dynamic leadership of which Leo is capable. If your love life has become a little stale – a major tragedy for your lusty sign – then Ruby fires up your enthusiasm for new relationships, or revitalizes an existing one.

RHODOCHROSITE

If expression of your erotic feelings has become blocked, or if your passion has waned and needs to be revitalized, Rhodochrosite encourages spontaneous expression of your passion. This stone is exceptionally useful for healing any kind of emotional or sexual abuse, and it is beneficial if you are repressing something in yourself that you do not want to face – this stone provides support while you gaze upon the formerly unacceptable.

crystals and your **way of thinking**

WATERMELON TOURMALINE

Leo tends to think in straight lines, and to be dogmatic. Garnet is a useful stone in that it enables you to let go of obsolete ideas. You expect other people to follow you and Watermelon Tourmaline encourages you to be open to someone else's opinion. If you receive constructive criticism, Kunzite opens you to the truth of this. Tiger's Eye assists you to resolve mental conflicts, especially those caused by pride, and it helps in seeing both the bigger picture and the minute detail. Topaz enlivens your mind and assists you to recognize the influence you have on others.

MORGANITE

crystals and your **soul pathway**

Leo is on a soul pathway of owning and expressing power while retaining humility and heart-centredness. The loving energy of Morganite (Pink Beryl) gently cleanses your heart, opening it to unconditional love and dissolving any egotism that may be blocking your spiritual advancement. Rhodochrosite represents selfless love and integrates the spiritual into everyday life. It teaches you that power flows through you, rather than from you, and that in owning your power, you acknowledge that there is really nothing to own. You become open-hearted and empowered (see Opening the heart ritual, page 105).

leo **crystal healing**

Physiologically, Leo is associated with the heart, the circulatory system and the lower back. Any sexual frustration you experience tends to physicalize itself as back pain, especially in the lower back. Use Ruby to attract an outlet for your libido and, in the meantime, place a Carnelian or Cathedral Quartz over the pain to release muscle spasm.

Bloodstone (Heliotrope) is useful for anything to do with blood, and is excellent for dysfunction of the circulatory system, while Rhodochrosite heals the heart itself. As you belong to a sign with a tendency to play hard, Golden (Imperial) Topaz is beneficial as it overcomes exhaustion, revitalizing your energy. Wear it for long periods, especially when deeply engaged with work or play.

leo **birthday ritual**

On your birthday, sit quietly holding your Red Garnet, bringing your attention deep into your self. Pass your crystal over the flame of a candle to cleanse and purify it. Holding your crystal in your lap, picture a sacred flame spreading out from the crystal to enfold your whole body. This sacred flame forms a cloak of protection around you and replenishes your vitality, giving you a calm centre. Its powerful energy ignites your creativity and power of manifestation. Now picture whatever you wish for yourself flowing out across the next year of your life. When you are ready, bring your attention back into the room and either wear your Red Garnet or place it in a position where you will see it often.

sun in virgo
the virgin
AUGUST 23–SEPTEMBER 22

BIRTHSTONES Sardonyx, Peridot

ABUNDANCE STONE Moss Agate

RITUAL STONE Moss Agate

COMPANION CRYSTALS Agate, Amazonite, Amber, Blue Topaz, Carnelian, Cerussite, Chrysocolla, Citrine, Dioptase, Garnet, Magnesite, Moonstone, Opal, Purple Obsidian, Red Tourmaline, Rutilated Quartz (Angel Hair), Sapphire, Smithsonite, Sodalite, Sugilite, Vanadinite, Violet Spinel, Watermelon Tourmaline

your virgo **birthstones** and you

You value integrity and virtuous conduct and your Sardonyx birthstone resonates to these qualities. Strong and stable, it supports your search for meaningful existence and assists in processing information. Supplementing your willpower it strengthens your character, enhancing your self-control. You want to grind things down until you reach the nub of the matter and Sardonyx facilitates this process. It also assists you to find a stable relationship, and attracts good friends.

Lighter and livelier Peridot, your co-birthstone, supports your razor-sharp perception. It assists in letting go of habits that block your growth, and encourages you to be kinder to yourself – an essential ingredient in overcoming your tendency towards self-criticism. Peridot's powerful cleansing action releases negative patterns and 'old baggage'. If you have done the necessary psychological work, Peridot rapidly moves you into a new stage of self-development and encourages you to look to your own higher energies for guidance.

crystals and your **potential**

Virgo has an enormous capacity to be of service to others, which sometimes means that your own needs and aspirations are put on hold. Wearing Blue Topaz ensures you live up to your own aspirations without reneging on your dedication to service. Blue Topaz insists that the scripts you live by are those you write yourself in accord with your own truth. It takes you out of the 'servitude trap', teaching that true service comes from the heart, doing what is necessary without thought of reward or recognition and yet, at the same time, not allowing yourself to be put upon by others. This stone aligns you with the angels of truth and wisdom, drawing their invaluable assistance into your day-to-day life. Your gifts of common sense and a rational mind, combined with an innate ability for organization and administration, give you the ability to plan things in the most functional way possible, making the world run more efficiently. You may find yourself taking a supporting role and carrying a piece of Orange Calcite facilitates a role commensurate with your abilities.

Many Virgos are gifted craftworkers. Celestite, while not directly a Virgo birth crystal, is strongly linked to Mercury and to the arts. This stone helps you to rise above the mundane to access intuitive creativity. Moss Agate is excellent for anyone engaged in agriculture or horticulture, helping you to work intuitively with the land. Understanding the nature of true health, many Virgos are drawn towards the healing professions. Crystals are holistic healing tools that support your abilities and Fluorite is especially useful in understanding the effect of the emotions and mind on the body.

crystals and your **challenges**

As a Virgo, you seek perfection and set incredibly high goals for yourself and others. If standards are not reached, you can become critical. Lowering your expectations to create achievable goals is a major challenge. Red Tourmaline overcomes the tendency to be critical. The problem with perfection is that it doesn't allow you to make mistakes but, with Peridot's help, you can admit to mistakes, accept them as a learning experience and move on.

crystals and your **emotions**

You have a somewhat prosaic approach to emotion. With the Sun in intellectual Virgo, you are happy to discuss and dissect your emotions, but not to actually feel the feelings. Moss Agate puts you in touch with those feelings and enhances your ability to express what you feel from your heart rather than your mind. The self-criticalness of Virgo may well leave you with low self-esteem and deep-seated emotional stress, and Moss Agate boosts awareness of your positive qualities and helps you to accept your true worth. Your sign has a reputation for prudishness, and yet, as an earth sign, you are deeply sensual. Vanadinite helps you to become comfortable with your physicality, shifting the emphasis from your mind to your body. This stone transfers the perfection of the highest levels of your being into the cellular structures of your physical body. Sexual activity becomes an expression of your own divine nature.

crystals and your **way of thinking**

You have strong mental abilities and a propensity for logical thought and categorizing, qualities that are heightened by the use of Sardonyx. This stone strengthens perception and aids assimilating and processing information. Virgo likes to analyse and you have excellent powers of discrimination, but you may well become so fixated on detail that you miss the bigger picture. Yellow Sapphire is an excellent stone for widening overall focus, while a Nebula Stone shows you the smallest particle and embraces infinity. Your thinking can sometimes be restricted by being too practical and rigidly logical, so heightening your intuition with Sugilite can be highly beneficial.

crystals and your **soul pathway**

The Virgo soul is on the pathway of altruistic service to others and this is facilitated by Lavender-Violet Smithsonite, which encourages joyful spiritual service. A barnacle crystal (many small crystals covering a larger crystal) is helpful for anyone engaged in

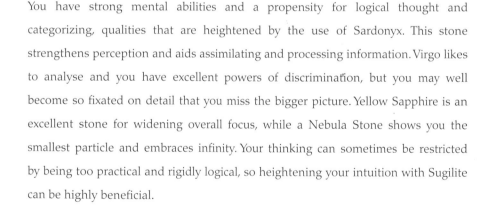

service. It enhances common purpose and promotes working together harmoniously. Barnacles are often found in combination with a bridge – a small crystal growing out of a larger. A bridge, as the name suggests, bridges gaps and brings people together. It joins the inner and outer levels, and brings life on earth more closely into alignment with your soul's purpose. Magnesite, a crystal that can look remarkably brain-like, assists you to remain in your own centre, standing by placidly while someone makes their own mistakes.

SMITHSONITE

virgo **crystal healing**

Virgo understands the causes of psychosomatic disease – the effect of the mind and emotions on the body. Sugilite enhances this understanding and goes to the root of dis-ease, while Moss Agate overcomes your sensitivity to weather or environmental pollutants, which can create diseases such as hay fever.

MAGNESITE

Virgo is associated with the intestines, spleen and nervous system, and tension or anxiety immediately makes itself felt in the gut. This can be soothed by Amber placed on the abdomen or slipped through your fingers during stressful situations. Dendritic Agate, with its delicate tendrils, resembles the nervous system and this is an effective stone for soothing, restoring or regenerating nerves and for overcoming the nervous tension to which you are prone.

SUGILITE

virgo **birthday ritual**

Sit quietly holding your Moss Agate, bringing your attention deep into your self. Touch the stone to the ground to cleanse and purify it. Holding your Moss Agate in your lap, picture a cord connecting it deep into the earth. Feel the earth energy rising up this cord to form a cloak of protection around your whole body, washing away your fears and refreshing your soul. Its powerful energy ignites your creativity and power of manifestation. Now picture whatever you wish for yourself flowing out across the next year of your life. When you are ready, bring your attention back into the room and wear your Moss Agate or place it where you will see it often.

AMBER

sun in libra
the scales
SEPTEMBER 23–OCTOBER 22

BIRTHSTONES Sapphire, Opal

ABUNDANCE STONE Sapphire

RITUAL CRYSTAL Apophyllite

COMPANION CRYSTALS Ametrine,
Apophyllite, Aquamarine, Aventurine,
Bloodstone (Heliotrope), Chiastolite,
Chrysolite, Emerald, Green Spinel,
Green Tourmaline, Jade, Kunzite,
Lapis Lazuli, Lepidolite, Mahogany
Obsidian, Moonstone, Peridot, Soulmate
Crystal, Topaz

your libra **birthstones** and you

BLUE SAPPHIRE

OPAL

Harmonious colours are important as they make you feel good, so the vibrant hue of Sapphire delights your heart. This beautiful crystal brings dreams to fruition, and imbues your life with lightness and joy. It aligns the physical, mental and spiritual levels, and restores the equilibrium which is so vital to you. This is the Stone of Peace, a quality that resonates with your desire for a tranquil life. There is nothing that your sign dislikes more than confrontation, and wearing a Sapphire assures peace of mind – and overcomes your chronic indecision. You are partial to a sybaritic lifestyle, valuing quality, aesthetics and good taste, and Sapphire's ability to attract prosperity is useful here. You feel happiest in a loving partnership and Blue Sapphire is associated with love while Green Sapphire ensures fidelity, and Opal faithfulness. Opal was regarded as unlucky but this is due to its tendency to shatter. Nevertheless, Opal amplifies traits, good or bad, so that you achieve the perfection you seek, and if negative qualities arise you will not appreciate having to deal with these. Your laid-back sign prefers ease to inner work, but if you have to face it, Opal smoothes your way, particularly as this stone stimulates creativity and releases inhibitions. This iridescent crystal opens the intuitive side of your nature. Your image is particularly important to you as you want to look good and to be thought well of. If your self-image is a little low, Opal enhances it and encourages a positive outlook.

crystals and your **potential**

Yours is a diplomatic sign with a flair for creating harmony, especially in your environment, and for finding creative compromises. It is in negotiation and conflict resolution that your potential can shine and crystals such as Blue Celestite support you in this. Lapis Lazuli assists in expressing your opinion on a matter. Sugilite supports overcoming conflict without either party having to compromise, and Ulexite goes to the core of problems, facilitating resolution and activating solutions. Chiastolite transmutes conflict into harmony, while Jasper supports during necessary conflict and Purple Fluorite turns conflict into co-operation. Dendritic Agate helps you to create a peaceful environment and Mahogany Obsidian supports your aspirations, removing blockages to your life's work.

crystals and your **challenges**

One of your greatest challenges is to avoid becoming a people pleaser. You back away from confrontation, and you desperately want people to like you so you put other people's needs before your own. As a result, your inner self is not aligned to your outer. Eventually, something has to give. Your own needs surface in a self-centred way and everyone, yourself included, wonders where 'that nice person' has disappeared to. Tiger's Eye, which draws your attention to your own needs as well as to those of others, can circumvent this problem. Nevertheless, as astute observers have noticed, you can be quietly ruthless in getting your own way, although you hide innate selfishness better than other people. To ensure congruency between your own needs and those of others, wear Mangano Calcite, a stone of unconditional love and acceptance. If you have become 'sugary sweet', Wulfenite will release you.

AQUAMARINE

PINK CARNELIAN

AMETRINE

BLOODSTONE

Your sign has a tendency to be judgemental, which Aquamarine overcomes because it has the power to promote tolerance of others. This tendency arises out of your strong desire for perfection. Mangano Calcite assists in recognizing that everything is perfect just as it is, while Pink Carnelian persuades you to offer love instead of judgement.

Libra is noted for indecision and sitting on the fence. You see all sides of the picture and consider everything carefully, but also have a fear of criticism. Indolence is part of your nature and, if this is holding you back, the vibrant energy of Carnelian will move you forward. If you need help in making decisions, Ametrine combines Amethyst's ability to unite spiritual insights and common sense, and to ensure that decisions are put into practice, with Citrine's ability to make you less sensitive to criticism and to impart the skill to steer situations in a positive direction.

A final Libra challenge is that of living in the present moment rather than the perfection of what could be. Living in the now is facilitated by Bloodstone (Heliotrope), which can bring your dreams to fruition.

crystals and your **emotions**

Everything about Libra is laid-back and emotions do not run deep; you cannot be bothered with such intensity. What you are deeply interested in is love, desire and eroticism, and your seductive Opal birthstone draws these to you in abundance. But, be warned, wearing an Opal intensifies emotional states – although it can also act as an emotional stabilizer. The gentle energies of Kunzite awaken your heart and attune you to unconditional love.

crystals and your **way of thinking**

As an air sign, you tend to use your mind constructively but may get caught up in indecision (see your Challenges) as you view all sides of a situation in an effort to find a perfect solution. Bloodstone reduces confusion, assisting you to think in present rather than in future possibilities.

crystals and your **soul pathway**

You are on a pathway of relationship, both to yourself and others. A soulmate crystal (two equal-sized crystals growing side by side from a common base and joined along one face) is the ideal Libra crystal. Attracting a soulmate, this formation helps you to be a separate person who is united in an equal partnership.

SOULMATE

libra **crystal healing**

Physiologically, Libra is associated with the kidneys and lumbar region and Jade is the kidney stone *par excellence*. It has been used to cleanse, purify and revitalize the kidneys for thousands of years. Fire Opal heals the lower back and kidneys, and can stimulate the sexual organs.

JADE

Libra is also associated with the endocrine system and with keeping balance in the body, and in particular with mediating the relationship between the endocrine system and the needs of the physical body. Placed directly over the pituitary gland – at the top of the head – Amethyst boosts production of hormones and recalibrates the endocrine system.

libra **birthday ritual**

AMETHYST

On your birthday, sit quietly holding your Apophyllite, bringing your attention deep into your self. Blow gently on the crystal to cleanse and purify it. Holding your crystal above your head, picture a pyramid of light forming from the crystal down to, and under, your feet. Feel celestial energy flowing down into the pyramid to form a cloak of protection around your whole body, dissolving your worries, and giving you a calm centre. Its powerful energy ignites your creativity and power of manifestation. Now picture whatever you wish for yourself flowing out across the next year of your life. When you are ready, bring your attention back into the room and place your Apophyllite where you will see it often.

APOPHYLLITE

sun in scorpio
the scorpion
OCTOBER 23–NOVEMBER 21

BIRTHSTONES Malachite, Turquoise

ABUNDANCE STONE Hawk's Eye

RITUAL CRYSTAL Malachite

COMPANION CRYSTALS Apache Tear, Aquamarine, Beryl, Boji Stone, Charoite, Dioptase, Garnet, Green Tourmaline, Herkimer Diamond, Kunzite, Obsidian, Red Spinel, Rhodochrosite, Ruby, Sceptre Quartz, Smoky Quartz, Topaz, Variscite

your scorpio **birthstones** and you

Malachite is an ideal birthstone for your Pluto-ruled sign as its intensity resonates with your own. Bringing about transformation at all levels, Malachite is especially effective psychologically and has the ability to absorb negative energy and pollutants.

Journeying through Malachite's convoluted whorls releases the mind and stimulates visions. It mercilessly brings to light anything that is blocking your spiritual path and assists you to access insights from both your subconscious mind and higher consciousness, and to share these with others. You have a magnetic personality and Magnetite's attributes of loyalty and fidelity reflect and reinforce these qualities in yourself.

Your empathic Turquoise co-birthstone balances the forcefulness of Malachite, bringing inner calm. This purification stone has a high vibration that enhances your intuition and provides protection while you explore spiritual and darker realms. It provides solace for the soul and enhances physical wellbeing but, beware, Turquoise has the ability to change colour when in the presence of infidelity and, despite deep loyalty to a partner, Scorpio is not the most faithful of signs.

crystals and your **potential**

You have the power of strong leadership and the ability to get to the bottom of things, and your sign goes where others fear to tread. Topaz is an excellent stone for accessing your own inner riches and for attracting helpful people who facilitate your pathway through life. Use the vitality of this stone to recharge your batteries and to link to the highest forces in the universe. Scorpio is sometimes so busy exploring the depths that you forget to look to the heights, which you reach by wearing Golden (Imperial) Topaz. Your abundance stone, Hawk's Eye, has the ability to soar above the world, widening your vision and focusing your considerable powers of perception.

HAWK'S EYE

Your ability to diagnose and see below the surface makes you a natural healer. All the healing crystals are excellent tools for you but Charoite is especially useful with its ability to enhance perceptive analysis and to ground the self into everyday reality. This stone assists you to bring about deep karmic and emotional healing both at a personal and collective level.

CHAROITE

crystals and your **challenges**

Your challenge is to master power in all its manifestations. Black Obsidian is helpful in this, but only if you are prepared for the depth of psychological insight it brings, and for the darkness it releases before transformation occurs. You may find the gentler Apache Tear (the translucent form of Obsidian) more conducive to controlling your power urges.

APACHE TEAR

Controlling the sting in your tail is another challenge. Scorpio's tongue can be lethal but you are as likely to sting yourself as others. Hiddenite (Green Kunzite) calms your verbal assaults. Intolerance and judgementalism can be curtailed with Aquamarine, while Dioptase heals the festering wounds and repressed pain that cause you to lash out at others.

LARIMAR

Your sign can be self-destructive and the spiritual vibrations of Larimar move you away from self-sabotaging behaviour and set you on a constructive pathway. If ambivalence about being in incarnation leads to suicidal tendencies, Smoky Quartz alleviates this, and releases fear and depression. Deep Red Garnet is helpful in times of trauma as it strengthens your survival instinct and brings hopefulness into seemingly hopeless situations.

RED GARNET

crystals and your **emotions**

Your emotions run deep – although these do not show on the surface – and Malachite assists you to understand and release experiences that cause you dis-ease or distress. Malachite is a toxic stone and your own emotions can be highly toxic as you have a tendency to hold on to resentment (see the Forgiveness ritual, page 117). Topaz helps you to forgive and let go, while Rhodochrosite teaches your heart how to assimilate painful feelings without shutting down, and assists in releasing repressed emotions. This stone is beneficial in any area of life where you are in denial. Snowflake Obsidian forces you to recognize ingrained patterns of behaviour, teaching the value of mistakes as well as successes. Smoky Quartz dissolves negative emotions and shows how to leave behind anything that is no longer serving you. Your strong Scorpio libido appreciates Smoky Quartz's power to enhance virility.

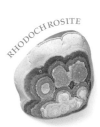

RHODOCHROSITE

Many Scorpios use sex as a weapon, or as a manipulation ploy, and any issues around this can be healed with the loving energies of Rhodochrosite, although this may take some time as Scorpio is a particularly resistant sign when faced with the necessity for change.

SNOWFLAKE OBSIDIAN

crystals and your **way of thinking**

GREEN GARNET

Your penetrating mind has acute awareness of other people's motivation, and their needs, and you do not hesitate to manipulate their minds to further your own ends. However, yours is a fixed sign and your mind unconsciously follows a pattern of rigid thought. It is virtually impossible for you to change your mind, but with the assistance of Garnet you can let go of outgrown ideas. Hawk's Eye dissolves negative thought patterns, assisting you to rise up to see the bigger picture, and Aragonite promotes flexibility of thought and helps you to consider different possibilities.

crystals and your **soul pathway**

Your transformative Malachite birthstone facilitates your journey into the taboo areas of life to bring back insights that can assist your own and other people's healing and growth. However, there is a need to go correspondingly high in consciousness and this is facilitated by holding a Sceptre Quartz, a long, rod-like crystal around one end of which a thick point has formed. The formation looks phallic, which is appropriate for Scorpio's intensely sexual nature, and it can transform sex into a vehicle for spiritual alchemy.

ARAGONITE

scorpio **crystal healing**

Physiologically, Scorpio is linked to the reproductive and elimination systems of the body. Thulite is an excellent healer for the reproductive organs, enhancing fertility when worn for long periods of time. Chrysoprase heals the prostate gland and fallopian tubes, while Topaz placed on the abdomen treats the testes, uterus and bladder. Beryl is helpful for disturbance of the intestines and can be drunk as an elixir to heal the intestinal tract. Place the stone in spring water and leave in the sun for several hours. Sip the water at intervals throughout the day.

SCEPTRE QUARTZ

scorpio **birthday ritual**

On your birthday, place your Malachite under running water to cleanse and purify it. Sit quietly holding your stone, bringing your attention deep into your self. Holding the Malachite over your solar plexus, picture a bubble of energy radiating out from the stone to surround your whole body. Feel energy flowing out from the crystal to form a cloak of protection around you. Allow the stone to absorb your negative and outworn emotions, giving you a calm centre. Its powerful energy ignites your creativity and power of manifestation. Now picture whatever you wish for yourself flowing out across the next year of your life. When you are ready, bring your attention back into the room and place your Malachite where you will see it often.

CHRYSOPRASE

BERYL

sun in sagittarius
the archer

NOVEMBER 22–DECEMBER 21

BIRTHSTONES Topaz, Turquoise

ABUNDANCE STONE Citrine

RITUAL CRYSTAL Red Spinel

COMPANION CRYSTALS Amethyst, Azurite, Blue Lace Agate, Chalcedony, Charoite, Citrine, Dark Blue Spinel, Dioptase, Garnet, Gold-Sheen Obsidian, Labradorite, Lapis Lazuli, Pink Tourmaline, Rhyolite, Ruby, Smoky Quartz, Sodalite, Snowflake Obsidian, Wulfenite.

your sagittarius **birthstones** and you

TOPAZ

Your birthstone, Topaz, provides abundant energy and promotes trust in the universe, teaching you how to *be* rather than do. For you, travelling is more enjoyable than arriving, and Topaz broadens your perspective and lights your path. Adventurous Sagittarius ventures further than many other signs and Topaz acts as a guide to the unknown. This stone's vibrant energy brings joy, generosity and all good things into your life. It facilitates the attainment of goals and supports your affirmations, leading you to discover your own inner riches. Blue Topaz is an excellent stone for showing you where you have strayed from the truth.

TURQUOISE

Your other birthstone, Turquoise, offers protection on your journey and attunes you to the spiritual realms. Placed on your third eye, the point between and slightly above the eyebrows, it opens your intuition and assists in stilling your restless mind during meditation. Placed on your throat chakra, it releases old vows and inhibitions, allowing your soul to express itself once more. Turquoise can take you back to explore your past, and this perceptive stone teaches that your 'fate' is actually created by your actions from moment to moment. An empathic promoter of self-realization, Turquoise helps you to understand that, ultimately, the answers lie within yourself. If you find yourself called upon to speak in public, Turquoise calms your nerves and facilitates clear expression.

crystals and your **potential**

Philanthropic Sagittarius is a sign that values (but does not always speak) truth and which is the eternal seeker after knowledge, and your Topaz birthstone connects you to your own inner wisdom and resources. It helps you to become aware of the knowledge you have gained through your life experiences, and puts this to work in the world. A natural teacher and philosopher, you have the gift of answering the great questions of life such as 'Why are we here?' and 'What does it all mean?'. Labradorite is an excellent stone for you. Its scintillating colours can take you into another world, stimulating your intuition and linking you to esoteric knowledge. With Labradorite's assistance, you can become a spiritual mentor.

crystals and your **challenges**

Your symbol, the centaur, is the only half-animal, half-human symbol. The major challenge for Sagittarius is to combine the instincts with the rational mind and leaven this with a liberal serving of intuition. Turquoise helps you to understand and integrate these different approaches to life.

Restless Sagittarius tends to live in the future; for you the grass is always greener somewhere else. Rather than stay and work at things, your impulse is to move on. If life situations seem to have you boxed in, and you have become despondent, try holding a Garnet for 15 minutes a day, or wear one constantly. This is a powerfully energizing stone that turns a crisis into a challenge. It fortifies and strengthens, bringing courage into seemingly hopeless situations. Charoite helps you to stay in the present moment, recognizing that everything is perfect just as it is, and this stone teaches you to find the gift in all that you encounter. If you feel at all alienated, either

from the world around you or from other people, wearing Charoite will ameliorate this as it grounds your spiritual self into the physical.

Tactless Sagittarius is prone to 'foot in mouth' syndrome, so learning to think before you speak is a major challenge. Red Tourmaline facilitates tactfulness while Malachite endorses taking responsibility for your own actions, thoughts and feelings if these are unwittingly being projected on to others. However, Malachite is ruthlessly honest in its perception and you may need to balance its insights with gentle Snow Quartz to help you think before you speak.

crystals and your **emotions**

Sagittarius is not comfortable with emotions. You might enjoy talking about them, but feeling them deeply is another matter, and you tend to talk them out of existence. With your habit of blurting things out, you may well have learned early in childhood that certain emotions were taboo in your family, which can lead to a blocked throat chakra. Unblocking the throat chakra can be facilitated by placing, or wearing, Blue Topaz or Turquoise at your throat. If you suppressed feelings because of fear of being judged or being thought 'bad', Blue Lace Agate comes to your rescue. This gentle stone counteracts the repression and encourages self-expression. Place it over your throat and heart chakras for maximum benefit.

crystals and your **way of thinking**

Your questing mind is incredibly active and can benefit from the calming effects of Labradorite. This stone energizes your imagination, bringing up new ideas. It balances analysis with inner sight, encouraging contemplation and introspection. Taking you to the core of matters, it synthesizes intellectual thought with intuitive wisdom, and reveals the real intention behind thoughts and actions. Your birthstone, Topaz, assists in solving problems since it sees both the bigger picture and minute details, recognizing how they interrelate. This useful stone confers astuteness and facilitates expressing ideas.

crystals and your **soul pathway**

Your soul is on a search for ultimate meaning and, with the assistance of Rhyolite, you can reach true knowing, while Sugilite has answers to great questions. Your soul pathway is facilitated by meditation, as many of the answers lie within. Gaze into the iridescent colours of mystical Labradorite, the stone of esoteric knowledge and initiation into the mysteries. In its clear yellow form, Labradorite connects you to universal wisdom and the highest possible levels of consciousness.

SUGILITE

sagittarius **crystal healing**

Physiologically, Sagittarius is associated with the hips and with the liver. Smoky Quartz is an excellent healer for these areas, and will draw off toxins from the liver if placed just below the ribs on the right-hand side of the body. With profligate Jupiter as your ruler, you are prone to overdo things and Charoite reverses damage to the liver from over-indulgence, while Dioptase regenerates the liver.

DIOPTASE

If your energy has become depleted, or you are suffering from burnout, the vitality of Ruby will soon recharge your energy and renew your passion for life. If stiffness has invaded your hips, Red Calcite removes the blockages that prevent you stepping forward in life, and, therefore, loosens your joints.

RED CALCITE

sagittarius **birthday ritual**

Sit quietly holding your Red Spinel, bringing your attention deep into your self. Pass your crystal over the flame of a candle to purify it. Holding your Red Spinel in your lap, picture a sacred flame spreading out from the crystal to enfold your whole body. This sacred flame forms a cloak of protection around you and replenishes your vitality, giving you a calm centre. Its powerful energy ignites your creativity and power of manifestation. Now picture whatever you wish for yourself flowing out across the next year of your life. When you are ready, bring your attention back into the room and either wear your Red Spinel or place it where you will see it often.

RED SPINEL

sun in capricorn

the goat

DECEMBER 22–JANUARY 19

BIRTHSTONES Onyx, Garnet

ABUNDANCE STONE Ruby

RITUAL STONE Aragonite

COMPANION CRYSTALS Amber, Azurite, Tourmaline, Carnelian, Fluorite, Galena, Jet, Labradorite, Magnetite, Malachite, Obsidian, Peridot, Quartz, Ruby, Serpentine, Smoky Quartz, Snowflake Obsidian, Stibnite, Turquoise

your capricorn **birthstones** and you

ONYX

RED GARNET

Yours is a serious and rule-oriented sign, enlivened by a strong sense of humour. Your Onyx birthstone provides the structure and authority you crave. This stone helps you to be the master of your destiny and has the added benefit of strengthening your confidence. It provides support in difficult times, and centres your energy in periods of mental or physical stress. However, Onyx can make you somewhat too self-controlled and 'heavy', and your other birthstone, Garnet, may be needed to infuse lightness into your life. Garnet is a revitalizing stone, bringing serenity or passion as appropriate. This stone inspires the love and devotion you seek from a partner, and encourages commitment and fidelity. It makes an excellent engagement stone.

crystals and your **potential**

You have a strong desire to be useful, with the ability to recognize what needs to be done, to organize it efficiently, and to see it through. This ability is supported by your Onyx birthstone. Many Capricorns have a powerful desire to get to the top. This desire frequently combines with an intimation of having a task to do, some duty or responsibility that must be taken up. The scintillating colours that flash unexpectedly from the dull grey of Labradorite reflect the brightness of your inner being, which is usually hidden behind a façade of conventionality. This stone aids feeling comfortable with your sense of duty and destiny, and enables you to put it to good use, while Amber links what you wish for to your drive to succeed.

With your superior mind, high principles and organizational ability, you are an asset to any business – although many Capricorns are called to law enforcement or government. Square-cut Garnet brings you success in business matters and develops your considerable leadership qualities. With your natural authority and desire to succeed, you are happiest at the top of the employment ladder. Energetic Ruby gives you the vitality to succeed, and promotes dynamic leadership.

When you have fulfilled your dreams, you turn to more spiritual matters. Azurite facilitates opening your intuition, guiding your spiritual unfolding and releasing inner wisdom. Gazing into a Fluorite crystal links you to the higher spiritual realities and at the same time grounds your spirituality into everyday reality.

crystals and your **challenges**

A major challenge for Capricorn is shifting from an outer- to an inner-directed self. Authority figures have loomed large in your life, be they parents, teachers, mentors or rule-makers of any description. You have lived by the collective voice of authority to which they all contributed. Your task is to find the inner voice of your self (see the Inner voice ritual, page 125) and follow its direction. Pietersite is a powerful stone for releasing mental conditioning and beliefs imposed by authority figures. Once you have achieved this shift from authoritarianism to inner authority, you can let go of your tight control on life. Your sign has a great desire for wealth and status. While Ruby can attract these, it never allows them to take over your life. This stone fills you with enthusiasm and confidence and brightens your pathway. Capricorn has entrenched principles, and you are concerned with justice. Fluorite can help to overcome a tendency to judgementalism and it is particularly beneficial when you need to act impartially and objectively.

crystals and your **emotions**

SODALITE

You like to have your emotions firmly under control and find emotional communication difficult, especially when it comes to expressing your feelings. Sodalite, while not a Capricorn stone, nevertheless is helpful to you because it encourages you to relinquish the control mechanisms that hold you back from self-acceptance and self-trust. This gentle stone brings shadow qualities up to the surface and allows them to be accepted without being judged.

Capricorn has a strong sex drive and your Garnet birthstone invigorates your libido and aids sexual potency, removing inhibitions.

crystals and your **way of thinking**

GALENA

Capricorn thinking tends to be somewhat rigid and in accordance with accepted credos. Galena, a lead-based stone that resonates with your stern ruler, Saturn, opens up your mind, encouraging investigation and experimentation, while Onyx offers the gift of wise decisions. The unconscious sabotage to which you are prone is removed by Garnet, which assists in letting go of obsolete ideas and ingrained behaviour patterns that no longer serve. Fluorite dissolves fixed patterns of belief, helping to move beyond narrow-mindedness into seeing the bigger picture. This stone organizes and processes information, linking into what is already known and assisting you to absorb new information. Fluorite also quickens your sometimes ponderous thought processes.

BLACK OBSIDIAN

crystals and your **soul pathway**

APACHE TEAR

Your soul is on a pathway of inner authority and power, desiring to live authentically from your inner self. Black Obsidian assists you in working for the good of society, and yours is one of the few signs that have the strength to handle the shadow energies of this powerful stone – but you may prefer the gentler Apache Tear, particularly as this stone removes self-limitations and increases spontaneity.

capricorn **crystal healing**

Physiologically, Capricorn rules the knees, skin and the skeletal system. Emotional resistance and mental dis-ease often results in stiff joints and this can be ameliorated with Stibnite. Fluorite is highly beneficial for the skeleton as it mobilizes joints, strengthens bones and alleviates arthritis. Placed in spring water in the sun for several hours, it makes an excellent elixir that can be sipped at intervals during the day. Stroked across the body towards the heart, Fluorite provides pain relief and heals the skin. Purple Fluorite treats both bones and bone marrow, while Calcite has a dual action. Taken as an elixir or placed over the long bones of the body, it encourages calcium uptake in bones but dissolves calcification, strengthening joints and bones. It also alleviates skin conditions. Aragonite mitigates joint pain, stimulates calcium absorption, heals bones and restores elasticity to discs. Aragonite makes a useful elixir for bathing affected parts.

STIBNITE

If your knees give you problems, try placing a piece of Azurite or Jadeite on them whenever you are seated. One of the most powerful healers for skeletal pain is Cathedral Quartz; place it over pain for 15 minutes. Amber counteracts your sign's depressive tendencies; wear it whenever you feel gloomy. Its bright energies are an excellent cleanser and soul-energizer. This powerful crystal draws dis-ease from the body and stimulates your body's ability to heal itself.

CATHEDRAL QUARTZ

capricorn **birthday ritual**

AMBER

On your birthday, sit quietly holding your Aragonite, bringing your attention deep into your self. Touch the stone to the ground to cleanse and purify it. Holding your stone in your lap, picture a cord connecting it deep into the earth. Feel the earth energy rising up this cord to form a cloak of protection around your whole body, washing away your fears and giving you a calm centre. Its powerful energy ignites your creativity and power of manifestation. Now picture whatever you wish for yourself flowing out across the next year of your life. When you are ready, bring your attention back into the room and place your Aragonite where you will see it often.

ARAGONITE

sun in aquarius
the water carrier
JANUARY 20–FEBRUARY 18

BIRTHSTONE Aquamarine

ABUNDANCE STONE Quartz

RITUAL STONE Angelite

COMPANION CRYSTALS Amber, Amethyst, Angelite, Atacamite, Blue Celestite, Blue Obsidian, Boji Stone, Chrysoprase, Fluorite, Fuchsite, Labradorite, Magnetite, Moonstone

your aquarius **birthstone** and you

Universal truths and brotherhood are important to you and Aquamarine supports these ideals. Many Aquarians live partially in the future, from where you bring back insights to assist the evolution of humankind, and Aquamarine invokes high states of consciousness that facilitate this transfer. It promotes spiritual awareness and service to humanity, aligning your purpose to your experiences.

In ancient times, this protective stone was believed to counteract the forces of darkness and to procure favour from the spirits of light. Its gentle, calming energy is excellent for reducing the stress to which you are prone. Encouraging you to take responsibility for yourself, Aquamarine also provides support when you feel overwhelmed by responsibility. If you are caught up in self-defeating programmes, this stone sets you free.

crystals and your **potential**

Your sign is here to help the evolution of humankind. You have the ability to see what will be needed in 20 years' time, and the skills to invent the future. Your potential, and your challenge, is to bring about social change and to fight for justice for everyone.

Always ahead of the trends, you are at your best in situations where you can use this ability to change the world for the better. Moonstone is a 'stone of new beginnings' that assists in your task, while Amethyst finds ways to put your vision for the future into practice now. Fluorite accesses what you already know, and links it into what is being learned.

The celestial vibrations of Blue Celestite take you into spiritual peace and contact with the angelic realms. It jump-starts spiritual development and urges you on to enlightenment. Labradorite is an excellent stone for developing your intuition and linking you to universal consciousness. Synthesizing intellectual thought with intuitive wisdom, it has the power to dispel illusions. One of the stones of transformation, Labradorite is a useful crystal to accompany you through change and to facilitate the shift into the Age of Aquarius.

If you feel that earth is not your natural home, the vibrations of Moldavite, a crystal from outer space, are helpful. This stone links you to cosmic consciousness and, it is said, to extraterrestrials.

As an Aquarius, one of your abilities is understanding vibration of all kinds, and knowing how to bring the disharmonious back into balance. This skill makes you an excellent healer and Magnetite, with its powerful magnetic charge, is a practical tool. It helps you to work with the meridians of the body and of the earth. This stone attracts and repels, energizes and sedates, and balances the intellect with the emotions to bring about inner stability.

crystals and your **challenges**

Your challenge is to remain flexible and open to change as your soul evolves. Belonging to a fixed and yet highly unconventional sign, it is easy for you to move out of balance.

Angelite and Blue Celestite realign you, while Magnetite counteracts nervous tension and increases your tolerance of emotional pressures. Fluorite helps any kind of disorganization and can be useful when your life seems to fly out of control. Your need to bring about change often causes conflict with the society around you.

Celestite is an excellent stone for conflict resolution, and Sugilite supports resolving conflict without compromise. Jasper strengthens you during necessary conflict while Purple Fluorite can turn conflict into co-operation.

crystals and your **emotions**

Aquarius emotions can be unstable and irrational. Moonstone is an excellent stone for soothing emotional instability and stress. A powerful emotional healer, placed on your solar plexus, this stone draws out and dissolves old emotional patterning. Emotionally, Chrysoprase instils a sense of security and trust. If you are in any way co-dependent, it assists you to be independent and yet committed to intimate relationship. Intimacy is difficult for Aquarius as you are much better relating to a group than in one-to-one situations. There are times when you feel alienated from others and the pink 'love stones' such as Rose Quartz or Rhodochrosite are extremely beneficial if worn for long periods of time.

crystals and your **way of thinking**

Aquarius tends to be a scatty, disorganized sign, although you are capable of highly productive, original thought. Your intuitive way of thinking may need some help in its organization, and Aquamarine is excellent for calming and focusing your mind, removing extraneous thoughts and filtering the information reaching your brain. It clarifies perception and sharpens your intellect.

Your sign is ruled by two very different planets. Saturn is fixed and rigid; it wants to conform. Uranus is eccentric, flexible and chaotic; it wants to change. You may find yourself pulled between these two polarities of conservation and evolution, resulting in a rut of eccentricity and non-conformity or to your desperately trying to fit into a conventional mould – with resultant mental stress. Blue Celestite helps to integrate the two aspects of your mind. It loosens up the Saturn side, and gently organizes Uranus, bringing the two into harmony, while Fluorite helps you to overcome Uranian chaos and bring about the reorganization and stability Saturn requires.

crystals and your **soul pathway**

Your soul is on a pathway of evolution for the good of the whole. Holistic Fuchsite is an excellent stone to accompany you on this journey, while Boji Stones resonate to a cause dear to your heart, the brotherhood of humanity. The stones, which some people believe to be alien beings from another planet, keep you on track.

aquarius **crystal healing**

Physiologically, Aquarius is connected to the shins and ankles, the circulatory system and the pineal gland. The pineal gland regulates the biorhythmic clock that stimulates production of hormones and the fluid balance in the body. Placed on the crown of the head, Moonstone is an excellent stone for the pineal gland, and also for the insomnia from which Aquarius often suffers. You frequently look – and feel – as though you are wired to an invisible electric current (the Uranus effect). Relaxing quietly surrounded by Amethyst points, point outwards, relaxes your body and mind, and draws off negative energy. Bloodstone (Heliotrope) has a powerful healing effect on circulatory disorders of all kinds and is excellent for cleaning your blood. If your shins or ankles require healing, skeletal crystals are helpful (see Capricorn, page 49).

BOJI STONES

BLOODSTONE

aquarius **birthday ritual**

On your birthday, sit quietly holding your Angelite, bringing your attention deep into your self. Blow gently on the crystal to cleanse and purify it. Holding your crystal above your head, picture a pyramid of light forming from the crystal down to, and under, your feet. Feel angelic energy flowing down into the pyramid to form a cloak of protection around your whole body, dissolving your worries, and giving you a calm centre. Its powerful energy ignites your creativity and power of manifestation. Now picture whatever you wish for yourself flowing out across the next year of your life. When you are ready, bring your attention back into the room and place your Angelite where you will see it often.

ANGELITE

sun in pisces
the fishes
FEBRUARY 19–MARCH 20

BIRTHSTONE Amethyst

ABUNDANCE STONE Bloodstone

(Heliotrope)

RITUAL STONE Blue Lace Agate

COMPANION CRYSTALS

Aquamarine, Bloodstone, Blue Lace

Agate, Calcite, Chrysoprase, Fluorite,

Labradorite, Moonstone, Selenite,

Smithsonite, Turquoise

your pisces **birthstone** and you

Pisces moves fluidly between everyday reality, imagination and spiritual mysticism. Amethyst forms a bridge between these. Highly intuitive and sensitive, with a tendency to absorb emanations from other people, you need Amethyst to cleanse your energies. It blocks geopathic stress and negative environmental energies that create physical dis-ease in sensitive people. Wear it at all times. Boundaries are a difficult issue as you are not sure where you end and someone else begins. This crystal is invaluable for establishing your own boundaries and feeling safe within them.

crystals and your **potential**

You have considerable psychic and artistic gifts and your Amethyst birthstone helps to open up your intuition, and to hone it. Beryl is the seers stone, giving great insight and heightening your awareness of hidden worlds. Use it wisely, especially its ability to manifest potential into reality. With your powerful imagination, if you fear the worst, you will manifest it, but Blue Lace Agate keeps you on a positive track. If you are a Pisces man, Blue Lace Agate assists in accepting your sensitive, feeling nature.

Your caring and sympathetic personality is drawn to helping others. Amethyst focuses your abilities and links them to divine love, putting them to the service of humanity. Your skills can be used in business and people management as well as the caring professions. Moonstone resonates with your intuitive nature and helps you to apply spiritual insights to the everyday world.

MOONSTONE

crystals and your **challenges**

Staying grounded is an enormous challenge for you. Bloodstone (Heliotrope), one of your companion crystals, has a double benefit in keeping you grounded and honing your intuition. Keeping out undesirable influences, it stimulates dreams and encourages selflessness and idealism. Best of all, it facilitates acting in the present moment.

BLOODSTONE

Most Pisces indulge in half-truths and escapism. Sometimes the escape is into fantasy, a world of wishful thinking and beautiful thoughts into which you slip whenever everyday reality becomes too harsh. Escapism is also found in a bottle, however, and addictions are common. Amethyst helps you to overcome escapism, taking you to the spiritual planes and opening a different kind of reality. Its ability to transport you into deep meditation offers tranquillity and constructive selflessness.

FUCHSITE

The most difficult Pisces challenge is avoiding victim-martyr-saviour rescuer-persecutor situations. You so much want to save the world, or just one person, that you give and give. You do not discriminate as to whether this is appropriate or not. Very quickly, you find yourself in victim or martyr mode. Fuchsite can help you to learn discrimination. Although not an associated crystal for Pisces, it is nevertheless invaluable for you. It shows how to do only what is appropriate and necessary for someone else, and teaches you how to stand by placidly while they learn their own lessons. Fuschite combines unconditional love with the tough love that no longer facilitates a condition. It overcomes situations in which you appear to be 'helping', and in so doing receive psychological satisfaction, but are actually facilitating the destructive behaviour. Morganite (Pink Beryl) is another excellent Pisces stone as it clears victim mentality, and Turquoise removes martyrdom from your psyche.

MORGANITE

crystals and your **emotions**

You belong to one of the most emotional signs, and may not be aware of your emotions as something separate from yourself. It is difficult to stand back and see your emotions objectively because so much goes on out of sight, in the depths of your inner feelings. Translucent Selenite clears emotional confusion and brings about a conscious understanding of what has been occurring at the subconscious level. This stone is a powerful stabilizer for fluctuating emotions. Aquamarine also gives insight into underlying emotional states and helps to interpret how you feel. It soothes fears and shields your emotional sensitivity. Sitting quietly with a piece of Beryl facilitates letting go of your emotional baggage.

Moonstone resonates with your intuitive nature and helps you to apply spiritual insights to the everyday world. It, together with Blue Smithsonite, aids in releasing emotional blockages and keeps your body and emotions in balance.

Pisces often moves on to the next relationship without ending the current one, and undercurrents from several relationships run beneath the surface. Meditating with an Aquamarine helps to see these links clearly, and the Tie cutting ritual (see page 101) assists in removing the hooks you have inadvertently left in other people as well as those they have left in you.

crystals and your **way of thinking**

Your thinking is extremely emotional and you often confuse emotion with thought. Many of your actions are actually reactions to feelings rather than reasoned decisions. Blue Lace Agate helps to distinguish between your mind and your emotions. It enhances your imagination and helps you to apply your intuitive insights rationally. Logical thought is enhanced by two crystals not connected to Pisces but nevertheless exceedingly useful. Kyanite cuts through illusion and confusion, increasing the capacity for logical and linear thought while at the same time helping spiritual awareness, and encourages speaking your truth. Sodalite also encourages logical thought, and unites this with intuition and spiritual perception.

crystals and your **soul pathway**

Selenite facilitates your soul pathway of union with the divine, and Magnesite assists in practising unconditional love, allowing the other person to be totally who they are without requiring them to change or being affected yourself by their difficulties.

pisces **crystal healing**

Physiologically, Pisces is associated with the feet, lymphatic system and the pituitary gland. Moonstone regulates the flow of lymph and Pietersite balances the pituitary, while Smoky Quartz is good for your feet, relieving cramps and, pointed away from the body, drawing off negative energy. Most Pisces dis-ease is associated with difficulties in being in a physical body, with soaking up other people's feelings and with the effects of excessive emotions and escapism. Lepidolite is excellent for dis-ease of all kinds and enhances standing in your own space, freed from the influence of others. It overcomes emotional or mental dependence and supports releasing addictions. Its lithium component controls mood swings and brings about emotional balance. It is particularly beneficial taken as an elixir. Place an untumbled piece of the stone in spring water, stand in sunlight for several hours, and then sip at intervals.

pisces **birthday ritual**

Place your Blue Lace Agate under running water to cleanse it. Sit quietly holding your stone, bringing your attention deep into your self. Holding your Blue Lace Agate over your solar plexus, picture a bubble of energy radiating out from the crystal to surround your whole body. Feel energy flowing out the crystal to form a cloak of protection around you. Allow the stone to absorb your negative and outworn emotions, giving you a calm centre. Its powerful energy ignites your creativity and power of manifestation. Now picture whatever you wish for yourself flowing out across the next year of your life. When you are ready, bring your attention back into the room and wear your Blue Lace Agate or place it where you will see it often.

CRYSTAL MASKS

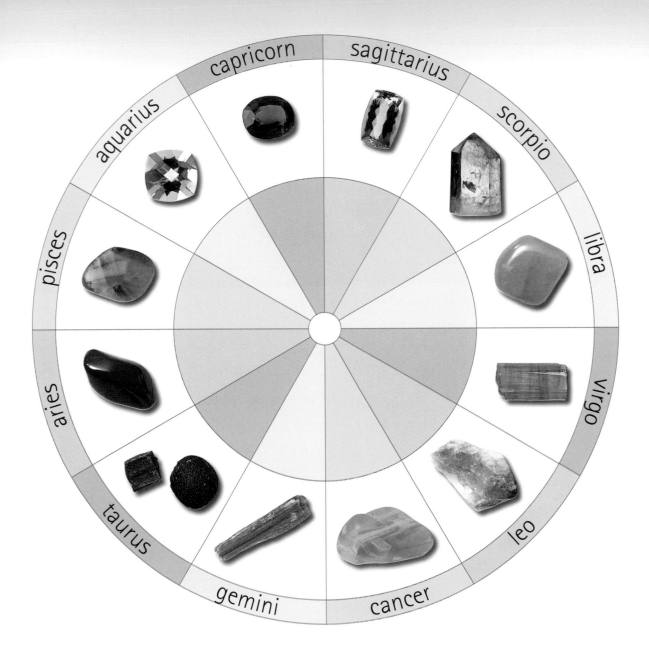

The point (or sign) rising over the eastern horizon at the moment you were born is known as the Ascendant. In ancient times it was believed that the planet ruling the Ascendant was a god or goddess who presided over your birth and oversaw the course of your whole life. Some of the planetary gods and goddesses, such as Venus or Jupiter, were beneficent and well intentioned – they were like fairy godmothers who bestowed abundant blessings. Others, such as Saturn, were hard taskmasters, but all planets had their virtues and all signs their positive qualities. Saturn, for example, rules a Capricorn Ascendant and is joint ruler of Aquarius, and offers the gifts of wisdom, resilience and inner discipline.

The Ascendant represents the face you present to the world – or the mask that the personality wears – and it can be very different to your Sun-sign self. If your Sun-sign characteristics do not fit, then you may reflect your Ascendant. If, for instance, you have a Virgo Ascendant, the world perceives you as an efficient person no matter how disorganized you really are. This Ascendant disguises a dreamy Sun under a veneer of efficiency, but, used constructively, it enables that Sun to be more organized.

Your Ascendant crystal is a powerful tool for self-development. Working with this crystal gives you confidence and makes the rising sign qualities more innately *yours*. Linking with the crystal manifests the blessings bestowed at birth by your fairy godmother. (If you do not know your Ascendant, see Appendix, pages 138–139, to find out.)

♈ aries ascendant

ASCENDANT CRYSTAL

Jasper

meeting the **world**

The face you present to the world, or the mask behind which you hide, is bold, brash and assertive. With a rambunctious Aries Ascendant you are a whirlwind of activity, knowing exactly what you want and determined to be first in everything. Other people often describe you as 'pushy' and Jasper, your Ascendant crystal, assists in pacing yourself, instils much-needed patience, and suggests how to put your considerable leadership abilities to good use. It gives you the determination to carry through tasks rather than abandoning them half completed.

Jasper brings out your courage in facing up to problems, and supports dealing with them honestly and assertively. Picture Jasper helps you to keep a sense of proportion, and ensures that, in your haste to be first, you do not forget to co-operate with others.

confidence **tricks**

Your confident Aries Ascendant can overcome the most timid and retiring of Sun or Moon signs. Carry a piece of Tiger Iron – an attractive combination of Jasper, Hematite and Tiger's Eye – to bring your hidden talents to light. This stone promotes vitality and is useful whenever you feel exhausted, particularly since that Aries Ascendant can 'burn out' quickly.

'fairy godmother' blessings

Courage, initiative and assertiveness are the gifts bestowed by Mars at your birth. Enhance these qualities with the gentle peace of Mookaite Jasper, which provides a useful balance between your inner and outer experiences, and balances the desire for fresh adventures with the need to complete your present task.

the aries mask

As the Aries Ascendant can appear so brash and independent, this mask is something of a double-edged sword. You may antagonize the people with whom you wish to co-operate. Or, from the outside, you may appear to be extremely self-sufficient or selfish when, in fact, you would welcome assistance and wish to co-operate. Combine Jasper with your solar and lunar crystals to soften your apparent egotism and allow your Sun and Moon to shine out. The Jasper will enable you to constructively channel your energies into joint ventures.

the aries ascendant meditation

Holding a piece of Jasper in front of you, walk briskly around the room tracing a wide circle. Breathe gently and focus on the crystal, gradually withdrawing your attention from the outside world and into your solar plexus. Feel how the Jasper enhances your courage while at the same time slowing down your impatient outer self and allowing you to move more harmoniously. Feel the strength of the Jasper travelling down your arms into your body. Sense how it strengthens your resolve, giving you the fortitude to see your tasks through to the end. When you feel ready, return your awareness to the room, then open the door and step out into the world with renewed stamina and vigour.

taurus ascendant

ASCENDANT CRYSTAL

Boji Stones

meeting the world

With a tenacious Taurus Ascendant, the face you present to the world, or the mask behind which you hide, is practical and methodical, but one that is loathe to change. People regard you as someone who can be relied upon, who will see things through no matter what effort that may take. Security is extremely important to you and your Ascendant crystal, Boji Stones, anchor you in the material world and promote inner security. Boji Stones come in female (rounded) or male (square protrusions) and a pair effectively balance male and female, or yin and yang, energies.

If the inertia of your Taurus Ascendant is dragging you to a halt, or compressing you into a rut that does not suit your Sun sign, then the forceful energy of your Boji Stones can help you to move forward into change. Use the male stone with its square protrusions to assist you to take the practical steps needed to alter your environment, and then the rounded female to regain the stability your Ascendant craves.

confidence tricks

Despite an appearance of good solid reliability, your Taurus Ascendant may cover a feeling of being out of your depth in the physical environment. If this is the case, Boji Stones assist you as they transfer their earthing vibrations into your body and promote confidence. They have the added advantage of removing blockages from your path, and revealing self-defeating behaviour you have adopted.

'fairy godmother' blessings

Endurance, pragmatism and good sense are the practical gifts bestowed upon you by Venus at your birth, but she also conferred a flair for comfort, luxury and good living. These qualities are supported by Boji Stones, which have an especially strong connection to material things.

the taurus **mask**

From outside, you appear to be highly dependable and this stoical mask effectively covers up the most flighty nature. Other people may make taxing demands on you simply because they believe you can cope, no matter how inadequate you may feel underneath. Boji Stones are an excellent aid to conserving your energy and bringing out the stamina of your Ascendant.

the taurus ascendant **meditation**

Hold the male Boji Stone in your right hand, and the female in your left. Put your hands on your knees. Breathe gently and bring your attention away from the outside world and into your body. Feel your feet firmly anchored to the floor, allow yourself to connect to the earth beneath your feet, feeling its nourishing and supportive energies flowing up through your feet and legs and into your belly. Move your Boji Stones to a point just below your navel. Feel the energy curling in on itself, filling up an empty space. This will provide a battery on which you can draw.

Now release your feet and stride forward walking lightly on the earth so that you flow to the rhythm of incarnation.

gemini ascendant

ASCENDANT CRYSTAL

Kyanite

meeting the world

A Gemini Ascendant is instantly recognizable because your impact on the world, or the mask behind which you hide, involves words and gestures. Most people with Gemini Ascendant talk with mouth and hands. With an insatiable curiosity, you report on the world, and yours is the multifaceted Ascendant that is the born salesperson, or the fixer.

A Gemini Ascendant tends to be jack of all trades and master of none. You are simply too interested in everything to spend time studying one particular thing in depth. Unless your Sun sign is particularly one-pointed, your Ascendant's superficiality can be a handicap – but the good news is that your Ascendant crystal, Kyanite, has the power to cut through superficiality to reach the core. It can also encourage your attunement to the universal mind, promoting spiritual maturation and personal integrity.

confidence tricks

Your lively and quick-witted Gemini Ascendant has little need for confidence tricks, although some signs might well say that silver-tongued Gemini invented the confidence trick. However, given your Ascendant's tendency towards little white lies, your Kyanite crystal helps you to be confident that you always speak truth.

'fairy godmother' **blessings**

The ability to communicate with anyone and everyone is one of the gifts Mercury bestowed on you at birth, together with the ability to talk yourself out of, and someone else into, anything. With your quick wits, lively mind and considerable versatility, you adapt to possibilities and make the most of them. These qualities are supported by your Ascendant crystal, Kyanite, which increases your capacity for logical thought and intuition.

the gemini **mask**

Your communicative Ascendant overcomes the most shy and retiring Sun sign, but you may well use words to put up a barricade that prevents other people from knowing who you really are. Kyanite deepens your interaction with the world, facilitating greater self-expression.

the gemini ascendant **meditation**

Sit quietly holding your Kyanite. Contemplate its ridge and blades. Allow your eyes to go out of focus and your mind to quieten. Raise the Kyanite to your third eye – the point between and slightly above your eyebrows. Feel the energy of the stone flowing into your mind. Allow the stone to attune your mind to the universal mind and the source of all knowledge, heightening your natural intuition and your ability to make connective leaps of awareness. Tell yourself that whenever you need to know, you will pick up your Ascendant crystal and it will provide this link to the universal mind.

When you are ready, remove the crystal from your third eye. Picture a shutter closing over the third eye. Bring your attention back to the outer world.

cancer ascendant

ASCENDANT CRYSTAL

Moonstone

meeting the **world**

A Cancer Ascendant meets the world sideways on. You are rarely direct, preferring to size things up before sidling up to your objective. This tendency can disguise a more straightforward Sun sign. Your objective may be concealed, but you are one tough cookie when it comes to reaching your goals. Your Ascendant is ambitious and uncompromising. When you do make your move, you act fast and hold on tight. Your Ascendant crystal, Moonstone, opens you up to serendipity and irrational impulses, and helps you to be more direct in your approach to life.

Like the crab's shell, your Ascendant gives protection but you have a soft, vulnerable underpart – the solar plexus, site of the emotions. You feel things very strongly here, other people's stuff as well as your own. Your Moonstone can give comfort and protection to this vulnerable place.

confidence **tricks**

A Cancer Ascendant puts up a tough front that covers any inner feelings of vulnerability and you can appear hard. Moonstone enables you to show your soft heart without being taken advantage of. Your Ascendant benefits from a cyclical withdrawal, taking time to process emotions and to dream dreams, with the assistance of Moonstone, and then manifesting those dreams in the outside world.

'fairy godmother' blessings

The gift of nurturing and homemaking was bestowed on you by the Moon at your birth, together with sensitivity and compassion. Your ability to make people feel comfortable, and to care about their welfare, is supported by the kindliness of your Moonstone Ascendant crystal.

the cancer mask

Although Cancer dons a mask of toughness and invulnerability, this is an extremely caring sign and people with Cancer Ascendant often find themselves becoming the social worker to the rest of the zodiac, or acting as an 'earth mother' who fulfils everyone else's need for nurturing. This Ascendant retains a mothering role (in men as well as women) long after it would have been appropriate to let go. Moonstone will help you to release yourself and to channel your empathic nurturing qualities into constructive action.

the cancer ascendant meditation

Holding your Moonstone to your solar plexus, allow it to guide you into the past to see what is holding you back. Wherever you feel a strong pull, especially if this is at an emotional level, breathe it out, let go, and move on. Allow the nurturing energies of the Moonstone to fill the empty spaces that are left.

When you are ready, remove your Moonstone from your solar plexus. Stand up and step forward with the awareness that, from now on, you will nurture yourself as well as appropriate others.

leo ascendant

ASCENDANT CRYSTAL

Citrine

meeting the **world**

Leo is an ebullient, larger than life Ascendant that enjoys holding court – or which hides behind a mask of confidence. People cannot help noticing you as you regally survey your surroundings, and, as you are a born performer, your penchant for hogging the limelight often exasperates other people. Citrine, your Ascendant crystal, is an excellent stone for bringing out the benevolent side of your sunny Ascendant, which other people find hard to resist. Your Ascendant is warm and generous, and the abundance of Citrine supports in sharing what you have, while at the same time increasing your wealth. This stone imparts a flexibility and openness to new experiences, which Leo Ascendant tends to lack. Citrine energizes every level of your life and is a powerful attractor of helpful friends and mentors.

confidence **tricks**

A Leo Ascendant has the gift of making you appear confident, even if you are not, and this can disguise the most timid of Sun signs. Your Citrine Ascendant crystal further enhances your individuality and self-esteem, and improves self-confidence. Citrine magnifies joy in life and instils a positive attitude. Use it to help you listen to others rather than talking across them. Holding a Citrine assists you to remain calm in the most challenging of situations.

'fairy godmother' blessings

Abundant joy, self-assurance and charisma were bestowed by the Sun at your birth, qualities emphasized by your Citrine Ascendant crystal. This energetic stone supports your warm-hearted generosity, drawing to you all the good things in life. It encourages you to develop your creativity and attracts prosperity and success.

the leo mask

A Leo Ascendant wears two masks, pride and specialness. People with Leo Ascendant often glow with a golden radiance, as though they are one of the chosen ones – or believe they are (your Ascendant can be egotistical). This Ascendant needs to feel special, which is why you enjoy the limelight – and resonate to sunny Citrine.

However, Leo pride can cause difficulties, especially for Sun signs with more humility. When your dignity is challenged, you retreat into a cold standoffishness which is far from sunny. Citrine can make you far less sensitive to criticism, and teach you how to laugh at yourself and your delusions of grandeur. This stone restores your benevolent self.

the leo ascendant meditation

Holding your Citrine, stand up straight, take a deep breath and drop your shoulders. Take a step forward and imagine yourself walking confidently on to the stage of life. Look carefully at the roles you play. Ask yourself if these roles feel comfortable at a deeper level, or if you have adopted them as compensation for perceived inadequacies. If you have adopted roles that do not suit you, put them aside. Use the power of your Leo Ascendant to find more appropriate roles for your unique and very special talents, but remember to take the humility of Citrine with you.

virgo ascendant

ASCENDANT CRYSTAL

Blue Tourmaline (Indicolite)

meeting the **world**

To the outside world, you are a coolly efficient person. The face you present, or the mask behind which you hide, is hard working, dependable and service-oriented, which is supported by your Ascendant crystal, Blue Tourmaline (Indicolite). This stone resonates with your sense of responsibility and encourages love of truth. Blue Tourmaline enhances your desire to live in peaceful harmony with the environment and to be of service to your fellow human beings. Cool in a crisis, analytical and detached, you have the flexibility to embrace change and the organizational skills to remain in control.

confidence **tricks**

Despite your outward appearance of organized efficiency, you may well lack confidence in your abilities and allow others to coerce you into support roles, or servitude. Many people with Virgo Ascendant find themselves, for example, serving as a personal assistant rather than the boss, and you are often drawn to nursing and caring professions. Blue Tourmaline is an excellent stone for you. Promoting self-confidence and diminishing fear, it inspires compassion and tolerance. Dispersing negative thought patterns, it suggests creative solutions and helps you to shine, and it enables you to speak out when necessary.

'fairy godmother' blessings

A razor-sharp, analytical mind, that has the ability to categorize and organize efficiently, was bestowed by Mercury at your birth, together with the gift of wit and intuitive intelligence. Your earthy Ascendant helps you to work in harmony with the environment, an ability that is supported by your Tourmaline Ascendant crystal.

the virgo mask

When Virgo wears the mask of service, it can disguise a more ambitious or outgoing Sun sign. This mask gives you dedication to a task, but it may conceal your true talents. Your creativity may also be blocked by more pragmatic calls on your time. Other people are used to relying on your efficiency and may ask too much of you. Wearing your Blue Tourmaline ensures that you fulfil your fullest potential, promoting taking responsibility for yourself as well as appropriate others.

the virgo ascendant meditation

Holding your Blue Tourmaline, walk in a spiral, moving from the outside world and curling deep into yourself. When you reach the centre, stand with your feet firmly on the floor, knees slightly flexed. Feel your connection to the earth and the supportive energies it offers you. Allow the earth energy to travel up through your feet and legs and into your belly. Holding your Blue Tourmaline just below your navel, take deep breaths, pulling the air right down into your belly. Feel it join with the energy of the earth, forming a battery of energy on which you can draw.

When you have completed the energy charge, retrace the spiral and walk into the outside world once more.

libra
ascendant

ASCENDANT CRYSTAL

Rose Quartz

meeting the **world**

Libra presents a charming but indecisive face to the world, and you want your surroundings to be both harmonious and stylish. People notice you because you are always well dressed in pleasing colours and fabrics, but they also notice your inability to make up your mind and the way you sometimes swing between two extremes. Your Ascendant is the 'nicest' in the zodiac, you get on with everyone and relationships are extremely important to you, but there is a danger of putting your own needs on hold in order to please others, and this may be the mask behind which you hide. Surprisingly, your equable temperament conceals an ambitious, and somewhat ruthless, heart that can be extremely selfish depending on your Sun sign, although you get your way by charm and misdirection rather than confrontation and demands. Your gentle disposition is brought out by Rose Quartz. This stone of unconditional love and infinite peace attracts and supports relationships of all kinds.

confidence **tricks**

Your Ascendant is usually more concerned with a pleasing appearance than with looking confident, but your Rose Quartz Ascendant crystal teaches you how to love yourself rather than giving all your attention to pleasing others. In enhancing self-acceptance, it brings you confidence in yourself.

'fairy godmother' blessings

Your fairy godmother, Venus, bestowed on you the ability to look good no matter where you are or what you wear. This ability extends to your environment, you can create pleasing surroundings anywhere and bring a harmonious ambiance to your world. Venus taught you to value beauty wherever you behold it, and she endowed you with peace-making skills and taught you the arts of diplomacy and conflict negotiation – and of love. Rose Quartz assists you to reach creative compromises and to maintain inner peace.

the libra mask

This insincere mask can hide an innately selfish nature, and a deep need of other people. If this is so, promises are facilely made and many disappointments follow. The Libra desire for perfection can take you into relationships in which you become entrapped. To prevent this, wear your Rose Quartz.

the libra ascendant meditation

Holding your Rose Quartz in your hand, place it to your heart. Feel the unconditional love flowing from the crystal and meeting the love in your heart. Feel how the Rose Quartz energy purifies and opens your heart. Let this love flow throughout your whole being, teaching you how to love yourself unselfishly. Now allow this love to flow out to the surrounding world, asking that it will go wherever it is needed. Finally, close your heart around a kernel of love to sustain and support all your relationships.

scorpio ascendant

ASCENDANT CRYSTAL

Smoky Quartz

meeting the **world**

Your interaction with the world is intense but impassive. No matter what is going on inside, your exterior is calm but your perceptive gaze lays bare other people's secrets, and yours is an Ascendant that often makes other people squirm. Stubborn and determined, this Ascendant conveys the power to achieve whatever you set out to do. Your magnetic personality pushes things through, or manipulates its way to the top, but you may well find yourself involved in power struggles with equally assertive Ascendants. A Scorpio Ascendant has a compulsion to explore all the taboo areas of life and all that is dark and destructive, indeed this Ascendant sometimes seems to be on a self-destruct mission. Protective Smoky Quartz supports your ability to see beneath the surface and accompanies you into the places where others fear to tread. It gives you the courage and insight for your own healing and that of others. This stone also encourages you to be less manipulative.

confidence **tricks**

Scorpio is an Ascendant that successfully disguises any inner lack of confidence behind an impassive façade. Carrying your Smoky Quartz fortifies you during difficult times, strengthens your resolve and teaches you how to let go of anything that no longer serves you.

'fairy godmother' blessings

Charisma, magnetic charm, a penetrating mind and a strong survival instinct are just some of the qualities bestowed at your birth by your joint rulers, Pluto and Mars. Yours is the most intense Ascendant and you have strong powers of endurance that are heightened by your Ascendant crystal. Smoky Quartz grounds you into incarnation and, at the same time, links you to the highest levels of the universe.

the scorpio mask

Your secretive Ascendant gives nothing away. The mask behind which you hide is impenetrable. This mask may lead other people to perceive you as cold and unresponsive despite, the fact that the Scorpio Ascendant can hide a deeply passionate interior. Emotion rarely shows on your face, no matter how involved you may actually be, and you may need to remember to voice your feelings to those who matter to you. However, Scorpio is known for being a charismatic sign, and this magnetic Ascendant has a façade that less libidinous Sun signs may find difficult to live up to.

the scorpio ascendant meditation

Holding your Smoky Quartz in your hand, place it over your pubic bone. Feel the energy of the crystal pulsating into your lower chakras, purifying and re-energizing the sexual centres. With each in-breath, pull the energy up your spine from the base until it reaches the top and flows throughout your whole body. Feel how this Smoky Quartz energy stimulates your creativity. Finally, lay the stone down and step into your power.

sagittarius ascendant

ASCENDANT CRYSTAL

Topaz

meeting the world

Yours is a restless Ascendant, prone to acting on the spur of the moment. The number of questions you ask is the first thing other people notice about you. The second is how often you put your foot in your mouth; this is a tactless Ascendant that speaks before thinking and needs the assistance of judicious Topaz. With your questing mind, you have an insatiable curiosity about the world and a deep need to find meaning in it. You are an indefatigable traveller and usually have a bag packed 'just in case'. You don't hide behind a mask, you merely move on. For Sagittarius Ascendant, the grass is always greener somewhere else. This is not the most organized of Ascendants; indeed you can be haphazard to say the least. But you have the knack of coming up with some great ideas, and innovative solutions, and you make an excellent and entertaining companion on life's journey, happily adjusting to new circumstances and meeting fresh challenges with enthusiasm.

confidence tricks

Your Ascendant crystal, Topaz, fills your life with abundant joy, cutting through any doubt or uncertainty. It sheds light on your path, highlights your goals and taps into your inner resources. This astute crystal imparts confidence by instilling trust in the universe and teaching you how to *be* rather than to *do*.

'fairy godmother' blessings

An insatiable curiosity and an irresistible sense of adventure accompanied you into the world. Ruled by Jupiter, you have a philanthropic spirit, and you are a natural teacher and philosopher, but you may have to reign in a tendency to overdo things. Your Ascendant crystal, Topaz, assists in discovering your own inner riches and sheds any negativity you may have picked up on life's journey.

the sagittarius mask

The mask you don to face the world is one of happy-go-lucky insouciance and non-commitment. From outside, you may appear untrustworthy, simply because you do not always live up to your obligations or promises. Topaz can help you to overcome this and a tendency to use half truths and little white lies to cover your tracks, aligning you with your innate love of truth.

the sagittarius ascendant meditation

Hold your Topaz to the right side of your head with your left hand. Allow the expansive energy of the Topaz to flood through your mind and to synthesize the two sides of the brain bringing logic into harmony with intuition. Allow your mind to expand and take you on a creative journey, be open to whatever wants to show itself, remembering that, for you, travelling hopefully is as important as arriving.

When you have completed your journey, place the Topaz aside and ground yourself in your body once more.

capricorn ascendant

ASCENDANT CRYSTAL

Garnet

meeting the **world**

Despite your air of authority, there is a certain greyness to the Capricorn Ascendant; your hair often turns grey prematurely, clothes tend to be somewhat colourless and you blend into your surroundings. Yours is an Ascendant, or a mask, with tight emotional control. You present a serious face to the world; this is the Ascendant that is born 'old'. With a strongly developed sense of responsibility, you feel that there is a task you must do or a burden to carry. The good news is that, as you mature, you grow into your wisdom and authority and, paradoxically appear younger.

Ambitious and determined to reach the top, you organize other people's life as well as your own and enforce 'rules'. As a result, many people perceive you as cold and stern. Garnet enables you to lighten up and enjoy life, and this stone is particularly useful when life is hard going and there seems to be no way out, as it turns a crisis into a challenge and brings out your innate strength.

confidence **tricks**

Yours is a somewhat gloomy, pessimistic Ascendant and Garnet opens your heart and brings out your self-confidence. This stone removes inhibitions and the need to conform. It bypasses inner resistance, dissolving ingrained patterns of behaviour or beliefs that no longer serve you.

'fairy godmother' blessings

Wisdom, dignity, natural authority and strong powers of leadership were bestowed at your birth, but your ruler, Saturn, is a hard taskmaster and you were also given strength, self-discipline and a desire to be useful in the world.

the capricorn mask

The Capricorn mask is one of strict control, an authoritarian face devoted to the 'oughts and shoulds' of life. This stern Ascendant can effectively disguise a much freer Sun sign, giving yourself a hard time, and causing other people to view you as cold and critical. Garnet helps you to express your natural authority with warmth.

the capricorn ascendant meditation

Holding your Garnet crystal, picture your life path spread out before you. (Allow this image to arise spontaneously, do not force it or try to control it. If you cannot see the path, sense it – you may like to walk forward as you do so.) Notice where the stumbling blocks and obstacles lie, and pay attention to burdens and responsibilities along the way. Ask your inner self to indicate whether these burdens are appropriate for you. If they are, ask to find a creative way to discharge them. If they are not, put them down and move on. Ask your crystal to show you how to flow around any blockages in your path. Allow a creative response to rise freely into your awareness. Put the crystal down, and step forward confidently.

aquarius ascendant

meeting the **world**

An Aquarius Ascendant is light years ahead of the rest of the world. Your far-sighted Ascendant can identify today what the world will need tomorrow, which makes you an excellent innovator and trendsetter. You are concerned to promote the brotherhood of humanity and work for its good – and many of your solutions are revolutionary. This brings you into conflict with more conventionally minded people who cannot conceive the necessity of your vision.

Yours is an Ascendant with a desire to be different; this may be in appearance or in behaviour, so you find it difficult to fit into society. Either you adapt, and feel inwardly rebellious, or you are the rebel who inwardly wants to conform, depending on your Sun sign. Aquamarine is a useful stone because it helps you to feel comfortable in your surroundings without compromising yourself. It dissolves any fixed, self-defeating patterns you have adopted.

confidence **tricks**

Your stubbornness and desire to be different make you stand out from the crowd, but this may cover deep insecurity. Aquamarine promotes self-expression and assists in understanding how you really feel. This stone offers you the confidence of knowing that what you think of today, the world will be clamouring for tomorrow.

'fairy godmother' blessings

With two such different rulers, your birth gifts are a mixed blessing. Unconventional Uranus imparts perspicacity, far-sightedness and the desire to rebel, while conventional Saturn demands boundaries, discipline and conformity. As a result, you often end up in a very unconventional rut but may equally be the catalyst for change. Aquamarine invokes high states of awareness that lift you out of that rut and enable you to serve humanity, or to change the world.

the aquarius mask

The Aquarius mask is often zany and eccentric but is equally likely to be remote and aloof. Many people with an Aquarius Ascendant feel like a scientist studying another species as they observe their fellow human beings. This Ascendant is much better at dealing with the mass of humanity than on a one-to-one basis.

   If you are trying to hide your true nature behind a mask of conformity, Aquamarine will help you to be more yourself without provoking opposition.

the aquarius ascendant meditation

Holding your Aquamarine over your breastbone, allow its energies to transport you into the future. Look at the qualities you will need there, the changes that must be made, and the steps that will enable you to move smoothly into that future. Bring the insights back, allowing them to flow into the crystal so that you can access them in the future. Then put the crystal down and begin to make the necessary changes in your immediate environment.

pisces ascendant

ASCENDANT CRYSTAL

Amethyst

meeting the **world**

Fluid and adaptable, your Pisces Ascendant flows through life unconsciously reacting to powerful emotional currents that sweep you this way and that. As a result, you make promises but cannot keep them as life moves on. Your Ascendant, or the mask you wear, has a soft heart and a sympathetic disposition. Unless the mask hides a canny Sun sign, it can mean you are a sucker for a sob story and will welcome the common sense and discernment that your Ascendant crystal, Amethyst, imparts. This crystal can also guard against a temptation to tell untruths 'so as not to hurt anyone'.

Yours is an imaginative, escapist Ascendant that lacks boundaries and rarely knows where you end and where someone else begins. You absorb other people's feelings, and it is easy for you to fall into victim or martyr roles because you want to save the world – or just one person. Fortunately, however, Amethyst acts as a protective barrier, especially to other people's neediness, and prevents people from taking advantage of you.

confidence **tricks**

Wearing Amethyst boosts your perception and helps you to feel more focused. It has the power to calm your emotional currents, bringing objectivity. As a result, you feel more in control emotionally and this gives you confidence.

'fairy godmother' blessings

You were endowed with a compassionate and empathic nature and many artistic gifts, but your ruling planets, Neptune and Jupiter, have a tendency to excess which can be controlled by wearing Amethyst. This perceptive stone enhances your intuition and brings out your poetic sensitivity. Strengthening your boundaries gives you the confidence of knowing who you are.

the pisces mask

A Sun sign putting on the mask of Pisces is immediately veiled from view, except for your large sympathetic eyes that form pools in which other signs drown. People often feel as though there is nothing to grasp. You may well use the outwardly empathic Pisces mask to relate to the world, but feel no real connection. Amethyst helps you to be more connected.

the pisces ascendant meditation

Holding your Amethyst crystal, gaze into its depths. Allow the intense purple colour of the stone to activate your spiritual awareness, opening your inner eye. Look through this eye into the centre of your being to find your true self. Take as much time as you need to come to know yourself, and then take your attention to a point immediately above your head. Feel your awareness rising up through the higher chakras until it reaches the source of your intuition. Draw this source down to the earth so that you can access it more freely. When you are ready, put the crystal down and step out to meet the world with perceptive insight.

HOW YOUR LUNAR CRYSTALS CAN HELP YOU

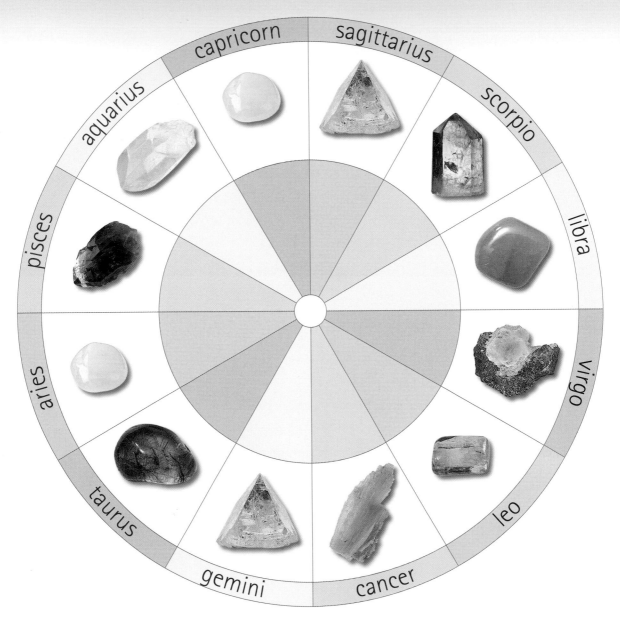

Spending two and a half days a month in each sign, the Moon has an intense effect on the psyche. If your Sun-sign characteristics do not seem to describe you, then your Moon is dominant. The Moon represents emotion and powerful instincts, patterns and ancestral or karmic inheritances that operate at the subconscious level. For all Moon signs, meditating with Bloodstone (Heliotrope) for 15 minutes at full Moon brings to light the unfulfilled needs and desires that are driving your life. These are 'old tapes' that you play internally, automatically reacting to triggers buried in your psyche. The tapes include past life experiences, parental strictures, hidden fears and the 'lunar food' with which you comfort yourself.

Once a month, the Moon conjoins its place in your birthchart. At this time, you are particularly sensitive and unresolved residues of the past surge to the surface. By attuning to your lunar crystals, you can reprogramme old tapes that are running you without your knowledge.

The Moon has a strong connection to mothering and lunar crystals can help to give you the nurturing that you need, removing emotional dependence and facilitating healthy sources of nourishment.

Each Moon sign has a crystal that develops your intuition. Intuition means listening to what you *know*, tuning into subtle signals that go beyond the five senses, pulling together disparate facts and leaping to a creative conclusion. Intuition offers insights and answers that cannot be accessed through normal channels. It is invaluable, and can transform your life. (If you do not know your Moon sign, turn to the Appendix, pages 138–141, to find out.)

moon in aries

MOON CRYSTAL Snow Quartz

INTUITION CRYSTAL Ametrine

LUNAR CRYSTALS Ametrine, Aragonite, Aventurine, Bloodstone (Heliotrope), Blue Lace Agate, Carnelian, Cerussite, Chrysoberyl, Chrysoprase, Hawk's Eye, Iron Pyrite, Jasper, Kunzite, Magnesite, Red Jade, Rhodonite, Ruby, Sunstone

your moon **crystal**

Snow Quartz has all the positive energy amplification properties of clear Quartz but it is much slower in its effect. This is extremely beneficial as it calms your fiery Moon and teaches you the value of co-operation and diplomacy. Quartz is a crystal that takes energy to the most perfect state possible and that acts like a natural computer storing information and energy patterns. It is extremely helpful in reprogramming the deep, ingrained behaviour patterns of the Moon, and has the ability to dissolve karmic seeds carried forward from other lives.

positive aries **moon qualities**

With your Moon in Aries you have abundant courage and initiative, strong ideals and plenty of stamina, and the ability to assert yourself forcefully. Others tend to follow where you enthusiastically lead. When you are centred in your self rather than your ego, you are capable of great concern for others, and will fight for their rights if necessary. Aventurine and Bloodstone (Heliotrope) are excellent stones to support the positive qualities of your Moon.

explore your **hidden needs**

You have a need for passion, freedom and adventure, which Ruby supports. You dislike being told what to do, or being given advice, and, with powerful emotional needs that demand instant gratification, part of you is still rather child-like. This headstrong part of your psyche wants to be admired and validated, and to be recognized for those special Aries qualities of courage and individuality. In pursuit of what you want, you can be single-minded and insensitive to other people's needs. But, depending on your Sun sign, you yearn to move out of that selfishness, to make contact with others, and open yourself to friendship and interdependence. Kunzite effects a creative compromise between your needs and the needs of others, while Cerussite promotes short-term compromise and assists in adjusting to situations to which your inner resistance is strong. Magnesite helps you to put ego into the background so that you can listen attentively to others.

CERUSSITE

With an overwhelming need to instantly gratify your own desires, and an ungraciousness that is born out of an inability to suffer fools gladly, your current desire is all-consuming. Being kept waiting or, even worse, being frustrated makes you feel physically ill. Iron Pyrite relieves frustration and boosts self-worth, bringing inner peace and the ability to set aside your needs for later gratification.

IRON PYRITE FLOWER

overcome **emotional blocks**

With the Moon in headstrong Aries, your attitude is 'me first, me always'. The old tape that says 'my needs are paramount' can be erased with the help of Aragonite. Programme this stone and keep it in your pocket, and put it under your pillow at night. It will help you to accept others as being of equal importance to yourself.

ARAGONITE

Impatience is one of the strongest tapes that runs you but, surprisingly for such an impulsive Moon, procrastination can also hold you back. This hesitation stems from fear of being criticised, of 'doing the wrong thing'. If this is the case, the bright, confident energies of Sunstone will quickly overcome your hesitation. The hidden part of your psyche is aggressive and angry. Aragonite combats this anger, promoting

BLUE LACE AGATE

CHRYSOPRASE

patience and acceptance, and encouraging discipline and reliability. Gentle Blue Lace Agate also heals inner anger as does the more vigorous Red Jade. This stone is appropriate when you need to let off steam as it releases tension in a constructive way. Hold it for a few moments, allowing your anger to melt into the stone, so that you can listen to the repressed needs that lie behind your rage.

Your emotional blocks are created from selfishness and self-absorption, which prevent you from being centred in your inner self, and your mental blocks arise from strongly held opinions. These blocks can be removed with Bloodstone and Chrysoprase, a selfless stone that facilitates recognizing the effect egotistical motives from the past have had on your development. Your opinions can be made more flexible with the help of Aragonite, which shows you the bigger picture. Passing the buck can be a deeply ingrained habit and the vigilant Hawk's Eye dissolves your tendency to blame other people for problems of your own making. It encourages you to attend to your own and other people's welfare.

HAWK'S EYE

nurture yourself

Rather than demanding flattery and respect from other people, which feeds your ego, you can choose to nurture yourself by self-validation and boosting your self-worth with Chrysoberyl. Fighting for other people's rights also nurtures because it harnesses your idealistic assertiveness to a cause you believe in, a process that is facilitated by wearing an Aventurine. Red or Peach Aventurine resonate well with your Mars-ruled Moon.

CHRYSOBERYL

develop your intuition

AMETRINE

Ametrine combines the elevated spiritual vibrations and protective qualities of Amethyst with the vibrant energy of Citrine. This crystal works extremely quickly, which suits your impatient Moon, linking you to higher consciousness. Ametrine releases tension in the head, calming your mind and bringing a greater focus to meditation. In the ensuing silence, you hear your own intuition at work.

your aries moon **past lives**

Your past life roles have included the crusader, the pioneer and the advocate for the disinherited. Aries Moon past lives often feature war, accidents and bloodshed. Wearing Carnelian keeps you safe while Bloodstone teaches how to avoid dangerous situations and shows how to make a strategic withdrawal so that you live to fight another day. It also ameliorates your chronic impatience.

CARNELIAN

Your karmic inheritance involves issues around self-centredness, and the need to distinguish between assertion and aggression. Wearing Jasper helps you to understand the difference between the two. In the past, you are likely to have been arrogant and self-absorbed. Holding Bloodstone for 15 minutes a day brings you the quality of selfless Self and reconnects to resources of courage and initiative that have built up over many lifetimes.

JASPER

co-operation **ritual**

To stimulate your ability to co-operate with others, you will need a piece of Snow Quartz. Hold the crystal in your hands. Allow your eyes to travel over its surface, seeing its milky smoothness and sensing the wisdom in its depths. Close your eyes and quietly attune to the crystal. Let its pure energy flow through your hands, up your arms and into your heart. As the energy reaches your heart, feel how it releases you from having to do things alone. Be aware of how it links you to people around you. Touch the crystal to your heart and then to your throat to stimulate your ability to co-operate and to promote tactfulness.

BLOODSTONE

Say, out loud: 'I willingly co-operate with others and welcome their assistance. I seek harmony with all around me.' Sit quietly for a few moments with your eyes focused on the crystal. When you have finished, wear your Snow Quartz or place it where you will see it often.

SNOW QUARTZ

moon in taurus

MOON CRYSTAL Rutilated Quartz (Angel Hair)

INTUITION CRYSTAL Selenite

LUNAR CRYSTALS Apache Tear, Beryl, Blue Tourmaline (Indicolite), Green Agate, Green Calcite, Idocrase, Kunzite, Kyanite, Lepidolite, Magnetite, Malachite, Mookaite, Peridot, Prehnite, Rhodonite, Sunstone

your moon **crystal**

Rutilated Quartz (Angel Hair) has strong, earthy vitality and is an effective integrator of energy. It helps you to release your hold on the past so that you can fully realize your life plan. This beautiful stone helps you to raise your eyes from the mundane, illuminating the soul and stimulating spiritual awareness.

positive taurus **moon qualities**

With your Moon in Taurus you are loyal, faithful and dependable, and you flourish in a stable partnership. Because you have a deep fund of practical abilities and common sense, your strength and endurance enable you to carry through whatever it is you set your mind to.

Green Calcite dissolves rigid beliefs from the past, enabling you to harness the strength of your mind and purpose to new projects. Your outlook is usually constructive and Peridot is an excellent stone for encouraging positive expression of your Moon qualities, while Kyanite encourages you to trust your innate intuition.

explore your **hidden needs**

You have an inherent need for security and for status, but your strongest desire is for an unchanging world. As a result, you hold on to people and possessions because these provide a spurious sense of safety, as does sexual contact (see the Tie cutting ritual, page 101). Prehnite facilitates letting go of material things. This stone connects to trust in divine manifestation, assuring that all you need will be provided.

PREHNITE

One of your deepest needs is to connect with your unchanging, eternal self. Rutilated Quartz can take you deep into your inner being to access your spiritual self, the only true security. Your desire for security shows strongly in your relationships. You depend upon a faithful partner and a stable relationship and Magnetite attracts love, commitment and loyalty, qualities that your Taurus Moon heart holds dear.

RHODONITE

overcome **emotional blocks**

Jealousy is one of your most powerful emotions and can be a deeply entrenched block as you rarely forget or forgive. If someone gave you cause for jealousy years ago, you apply it to the present even though circumstances will have changed. Peridot is excellent for relieving jealousy, it takes you back into the past so that you can recognize what the experience has taught you, and teaches you how to forgive.

APACHE TEAR

If you stick with habits that are familiar and comforting but which no longer serve you, a Taurus Moon trait, or suffer from possessiveness, then wearing Peridot can reprogramme your security tapes. The Taurus Moon can be extremely fixed, clinging determinedly to the past and the way things have always been. You are the original immovable object and your resistance to change is so marked that you become physically ill rather than move on from a situation that no longer serves you, and are likely to blame other people for the problem rather than own it. To erase your old tapes, you need to recognize the part you have played and see how much you have blamed on others. The penetrating insights of Malachite take you to the heart of such matters, but you may need to balance this relentless stone with the gentle energies of Rhodonite, to work on forgiveness and letting go. One of the most

MOOKAITE

powerful emotional blocks that you have arises from holding on to resentment. Peridot and Rhodonite will help to release this and to open your heart to forgiveness (see the Letting go ritual, page 93). An Apache Tear can shed light on long-held grievances and release these.

GREEN AGATE

Mookaite imparts a desire for new experiences and assists with choosing the right pathway. Emotional flexibility can be provided by Green Agate, and meditating with Beryl will help you to shed your emotional baggage. Simply let it flow into the stone and then cleanse the Beryl under running water.

LEPIDOLITE

With the Moon in Taurus, you have a tendency to repress your feelings and, as a sexy earth sign, you need to release them physically. If you do not receive emotional and sexual satisfaction, there is always the possibility of comfort eating and eating disorders. This is especially so if you use food to 'stuff down' your emotions. Lepidolite is an excellent stone to assist with deep emotional healing and releasing dependency.

nurture yourself

BLUE TOURMALINE

Keeping your body warm, safe and comfortable is highly nurturing for you, as is sex. You have a strong affinity with the earth and going out into nature is one of the quickest ways to nurture yourself. Blue Tourmaline (Indicolite) connects you to natural energies and encourages living in harmony with nature, nurturing your physical body and your soul. This protective stone prevents negativity from sticking to you.

develop your **intuition**

SELENITE PILLAR

The delicate striations of Selenite lift you to another dimension, helping to move beyond the denseness of earth, taking you into the space between light and matter. This beautiful stone instils a deep sense of peace, opening your intuitive mind. This crystal carries the vibration of all that has and will happen in the world and is extremely useful for accessing the plan made for your present life prior to your birth. It pinpoints lessons and shows how they can best be resolved.

your taurus moon **past lives**

Your past life roles have included the tiller of the soil, the artisan, the craftsperson and, quite possibly, the medium. Many Taurus Moon past lives have centred around materialism and security. You may have suppressed your opinions in the interests of maintaining the status quo. If courage in speaking out is needed, Blue Kyanite helps you to find your voice. Kyanite assists in moving beyond the notion of a fixed and blind fate, leading you to take responsibility for the course of your life. The tranquillity of Kunzite connects to universal love and to the eternal spiritual self that resides within you. It overcomes the attachment to material things that has provided an illusion of safety in the past

KYANITE

KUNZITE

letting go **ritual**

To let go you will need a large piece of Green Calcite. Hold it in your hands and feel its waxy smoothness gently soothing you. Close your eyes and quietly attune to the crystal. Let its uplifting energy flow through your hands, up your arms and into your solar plexus. As the energy reaches your solar plexus, feel it soften and open. Touch the crystal to your solar plexus and allow it to absorb your fears and insecurities.

GREEN CALCITE

Bring to mind the person, thought, emotion or situation of which you need to let go. Feel your solar plexus softening and letting go, releasing that which no longer serves you into the crystal, setting you free. As the crystal absorbs this, say out loud: 'I let go of .... I release .... For my highest good.'

Then feel the energy of the crystal flowing into your solar plexus, bringing you comfort and a sense of inner security. Allow the stone to enhance your trust in yourself. When you have finished, place the crystal under running water for 15 minutes to cleanse it. Then place it where you can see it.

moon in gemini

your moon **crystal**

Apophyllite is a powerful vibrational transmitter that links the physical and spiritual realms, stimulating your intuition and conveying the gift of clear sight, enabling information to be received. An effective stress releaser, this stone calms your hyperactive mind and alleviates nervous tension. It promotes introspection and assists you to recognize your own true self.

positive gemini **moon qualities**

With your Moon in Gemini you are an excellent communicator who takes a flexible approach to life. You have the knack of knowing exactly the person who can help in a given situation, and networking is your forte. Your intuition is strong and you have the ability to make inspired connections and a tendency to do several things at once. Placing a Blue Selenite on your forehead assists you in shutting off the chattering mind and enhances your ability to get quickly to the core of a problem. Tourmaline is an excellent support for your positive qualities, and it has the added advantage of preventing you from flying off in too many directions at once.

explore your **hidden needs**

With the Moon in Gemini, your greatest need is to be heard – even when you have nothing of value to say. You may well fear your emotions, having learned in the past to cut off from painful feelings, and will rationalize or talk them out of existence, but you need to accept these feelings. Calcite stabilizes your butterfly mind and allows you to express your deeper feelings. If there are painful feelings to be healed, this can be facilitated with gentle Rhodochrosite.

Your instinct is to be emotionally uncommitted as you want to be free to explore all possibilities, and this is a fickle, changeable Moon given to guile and cunning manipulation of other people's feelings. Pink Carnelian will assist with committing to a relationship, bringing the emotional intimacy that you need, and it can ameliorate emotional manipulation and overcome the effects of previous abuse. This stone helps to articulate your feelings, and to find a companion who resonates on an intellectual level. You will not be happy in a relationship unless there is a meeting of minds. This is more important to you than emotional rapport.

You have an overactive mind that constantly probes and questions. You need to know. But this need may be so overwhelming, and so superficial, that you never actually find out. Sapphire focuses and calms the mind, releasing unwanted thoughts and mental tension, allowing you to focus on what is important. It is an excellent stone for communication at all levels.

Unconsciously, you seek social acceptance and have a need to be liked, and are not above adjusting the truth to what you think people want to hear. Ruby can help you feel comfortable in a social setting without having to seek approval, and Charoite assists in blending into your surroundings and having self-acceptance.

overcome **emotional blocks**

Blue Topaz is an extremely appropriate stone for the Gemini Moon. It overcomes a tendency to take liberties with inconvenient facts or to use white lies to avoid emotional hassle. This stone helps you to recognize the scripts you have been living

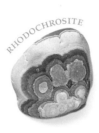

by and to identify where you have strayed from your own truth. Holding it for 15 minutes can help to erase old tapes and to reprogramme yourself towards truth.

The blades of Kyanite help to speak your truth, cutting through fears and blockages at the emotional or mental level. Snowflake Obsidian can help to recognize and release the stressful mental patterns and 'wrong thinking' that you mistake for emotions.

Gemini Moon often creates an emotional block by playing the role of puer, the Peter Pan figure who never grows up and who, apparently, slips through life without a care. With the puer Moon you remain forever young at heart, charming everyone but attached to no one. You rarely trust your own emotions, let alone those of other people. Emotional maturity is facilitated by Rhodochrosite, as it helps you to accept that emotions you were taught in the past to regard as unacceptable are, in fact, natural. This stone sets free your erotic urges and encourages expression of your passion in life.

nurture yourself

Mental stimulation and attention from others provide vicarious nurturing, and these can become your substitute for emotional satisfaction. You frequently mistake a conversation for an intimate experience. To truly nurture yourself, gaze into the depths of the Stone of Truth, Apophyllite. It connects to the angels of truth and wisdom, and to your own self. It is communicating with your self that gives you true nurturing.

develop your **intuition**

Aqua Aura is a beautiful stone that resonates with the Gemini Moon to activate your soul energy. It deepens your spiritual attunement and focuses your considerable intuition into constructive channels. Use it for quiet moments of meditation and centering. If mind chatter is a problem, Blue Selenite or Rhomboid Calcite will switch this off to allow your inner voice to speak.

your gemini moon **past lives**

Gemini Moon past life roles have included the communicator, the orator, the fixer and the salesperson. Your previous lives have centred around teaching and communication, but may also have encompassed gossip and satire. Your rise in life could have been swift, but not entirely honest, as there was a tendency to pull strings and manipulate your way to the top, and you may well have taken liberties with the truth. Unfortunately, you could have taken advantage of those less clever than yourself and may need to forgive yourself (see the Forgiveness ritual on page 117).

If you taught ideas that you did not fully believe in, then Variscite helps you to unravel the causes of any resultant dis-ease. If an over-emphasis on the mind, or a less than truthful tongue, in former incarnations has led to present life conditions such as dyslexia or speech impediments, Black Tourmaline, Sugilite and Royal Sapphire can assist. Aventurine is particularly effective for stammering or severe neuroses. These stones can be worn for long periods.

truth **ritual**

If you need to know the truth of a matter, the Stone of Truth, Apophyllite can help you. Before you go to bed, sit quietly, holding an Apophyllite pyramid in your hands. Gaze deep into its infinite crystalline depths and attune to universal truth. Picture in your mind an old-fashioned pair of scales, with two pans. (If you have difficulty visualizing, you can use actual scales.) On one side place the Stone of Truth. On the other side place the question or situation about which you need to know the truth (write it on a piece of paper if using actual scales).

SUGILITE

Now say, out loud: 'I call upon the Stone of Truth to show me the truth of this situation within 24 hours.'

Place the stone under your pillow and tell yourself that you will remember your dreams. It may be that the answer will come to you in a dream, or that it will become clear during the course of the next day. Be alert for a subtle clue; the answer may arrive in an unexpected way.

APOPHYLLITE

moon in cancer

MOON CRYSTAL Anhydrite

INTUITION CRYSTAL Moonstone

LUNAR CRYSTALS Carnelian, Chalcedony, Chrysocolla, Chrysoprase, Dioptase, Howlite, Jade, Jasper, Moonstone, Morganite (Pink Beryl), Opal, Petalite, Pink Tourmaline, Rhodonite, Selenite, Sodalite, Sunstone

your moon **crystal**

ANHYDRITE

Anhydrite's translucent surface is the colour of the lunar night. Physically, Anhydrite is an excellent crystal for you as it assists in controlling the fluid balance within your body and dispersing the oedema to which you are prone. Spiritually, this stone helps you to reconnect with your soul and to reach higher states of awareness. This powerful stone releases your attachment to the past.

positive cancer **moon qualities**

PINK CHALCEDONY

The Cancer Moon is an extremely caring and nurturing Moon with a strong family orientation and unanswering loyalty. You have the innate ability to empathize with other people's feelings, and to meet their emotional needs.

Your intuitive Moon acts as a mirror that reflects people's feelings back to them so that they can see them more objectively and therefore understand them better. As you may be a compulsive nurturer and care-giver, Chalcedony helps you to care about, rather than for, others and Pink Chalcedony in particular supports your kindliness and empathic qualities. Your powerful imagination is enhanced by your intuition crystal, Moonstone.

explore your **hidden needs**

Cancer Moon is powerfully linked to the home and a secure home base is essential since you feel unable to function without it. Like a crab, you carry your home on your back, accompanied by your treasured possessions, wherever you go. Tranquil Chrysocolla brings stability to your home and emotions, and Jade is a useful stone for safeguarding your possessions.

A need for emotional security motivates your behaviour, and you can be extremely possessive as you cling to the past. Pink Tourmaline facilitates letting go, and prevents emotional overload. Yours is a moody, difficult Moon and you hide an inner vulnerability with a hard shell, but this unnecessary defence mechanism can be transformed with Sodalite, which ameliorates your extreme sensitivity.

Your Moon is connected to mothering and nurturing. However, beneath your desire to nurture others lies a need to be nurtured yourself. Jasper supports in giving yourself the care you need. Morganite (Pink Beryl) assists you in recognizing your unfulfilled emotional needs and unexpressed feelings, while Selenite connects to subconscious feelings and powerful instincts, stabilizing your emotions and releasing you from the pull of your instincts. Moonstone is attuned to the astronomical Moon, a body which has a strong impact on your life, teaching the value of a cyclical withdrawal to process your emotions and dream your dreams, and then to emerge again and make those dreams a reality.

overcome **emotional blocks**

Many of your blockages and old tapes relate to your determination to cling tightly to what you hold dear. Yours can be a suffocating, smothering love and Rhodonite helps you to practise unconditional love. Cutting the emotional apron strings can be beneficial (see the Tie cutting ritual, page 101). Your inner lack of security has its roots in the unmet needs of childhood. Such needs result in dependence or co-dependence, which can be healed with Chrysoprase. Anhydrite releases your ingrained hankering after the past and Carnelian stops you living in the past,

promoting acceptance of life cycles. Citrine makes you less sensitive to criticism and helps you to look forward to the future. Cancer Moon is prone to self-pity and gentle Morganite releases this tendency, while Dioptase releases the need to control other people.

nurture yourself

You crave emotional sustenance and validation of your strong feelings. Rather than seeking these from outside yourself, meditate daily with nurturing Jasper.

develop your intuition

Moonstone enhances psychic abilities and develops clairvoyance (clear sight). It is also beneficial in helping to accept your psychic gifts. It has the facility to make the unconscious conscious, and to build empathy. At the time of the full Moon, when Moonstone is at its most potent, it encourages lucid dreaming.

your cancer moon past lives

Your past life roles have included the homemaker, the mother, the midwife, the wise woman and the cook, and anything linked to the sea. Yours is a sensitive Moon sign that is unconsciously coloured by the past. Emotional pain has created a vulnerability that you conceal beneath a hard shell of apparent indifference. As a result, you have a strongly developed sense of self-preservation and a great need for security. Your previous lives may well include over-dependence and emotional enmeshment. Sunstone helps to remove ties that attach you to parents, children or lovers from other lives (see Tie cutting ritual, opposite).

If you need to explore your entrenched but unconscious emotions, Opal can assist. It teaches you how to take responsibility for how you feel on a day-to-day basis. Howlite exposes the past life causes of turbulent present life emotions, releasing the strings that tie old emotions into the present life. Petalite, an expensive but highly effective crystal, gently clears negative emotions and cuts off any manipulation that is occurring through your emotional sensitivity.

Petalite is extremely beneficial in karmic work as it severs ties to people from past lives, working at the higher self level to promote the good of all. It is excellent for healing ancestral and family patterns because it reaches back to a time before the dysfunction arose and allows you to move forward from this space, healing the dysfunctional emotions of the ancestral line as you do so.

tie cutting **ritual**

This ritual does not cut off unconditional love between you and another person, but it does remove 'hooks' that drain your energy. These 'hooks' exist at subtle levels and may be found in the chakras or the aura (the biomagnetic sheath and its linkage points that surround your physical body).

You will need a large piece of Sunstone. Hold the Sunstone in your left hand and sweep it around your body. As you do so feel its joyful energy flooding through you and gently releasing any hooks that are attached. As the hooks are released, so the Sunstone seals your aura with healing light. Then use your right hand to sweep the remaining parts of your body, going over your head and below your feet.

Place the Sunstone on the crown of your head (the crown chakra). Ask that it will release any hooks from this chakra and replace them with light. Slowly move the Sunstone down to behind first one ear and then another, again asking that the hooks will be removed. As you move the Sunstone back up over your head, ask that any mental hooks will be released. Each time asking for the hooks to be removed, take the Sunstone to your third eye, located above and between your eyebrows, then to your throat, heart and solar plexus. Place the Sunstone just below your navel, and then at the base of your pubic bone to draw out sexual hooks.

Say out loud: 'I release all connections that no longer serve me, heal the places where they were lodged and return all hooks to their source. I take back any hooks I have left in other people and release them to their own pathway.' Then place the Sunstone under running water for 15 minutes to cleanse it.

moon in leo

MOON CRYSTAL Hiddenite
(Green Kunzite)

INTUITION CRYSTAL Yellow Calcite

LUNAR CRYSTALS Ametrine,
Apophyllite, Aventurine, Brown Opal,
Calcite, Carnelian, Chrysocolla, Citrine,
Dioptase, Fuchsite, Kunzite, Larimar,
Morganite (Pink Beryl), Rhodochrosite,
Rose Quartz, Tiger's Eye, Topaz,

your moon **crystal**

HIDDENITE

Hiddenite (the yellow-green form of Kunzite) is an excellent stone for your grandiose Moon as it emphasizes the positive aspects of your personality and promotes humility, while at the same time enhancing expression of your personal power. This rejuvenating crystal provides encouragement in difficult life circumstances and should be worn constantly to rejuvenate your energies.

positive leo **moon qualities**

TOPAZ

When the Moon in Leo expresses itself positively, you are generous, affectionate and warm hearted with strong loyalty. You spread your benevolence over everyone with whom you come into contact. You naturally attract people and, with an innate authority, are a competent organizer. This Moon is charismatic, confident, creative and vital, and your positive qualities are heightened by the vibrant energies of Topaz, which makes you an excellent mentor. Your deeply embedded loyalty can mean you stay in the wrong job or a destructive relationship for far too long, and your tendency to make sacrifices on behalf of others can be tuned to more constructive use by the transformative energy of Ametrine.

explore your **hidden needs**

When the Moon is in Leo your strongest needs are for personal empowerment and a feeling of being special. You want to be looked up to, adored and obeyed. To achieve this, you may resort to emotional games and manipulation, and if you are ignored, you retreat into wounded dignity. You also have a deep desire for luxury and self-indulgence. Finding your own inner specialness (see Nurture yourself, page 104) is essential if you are to bring out the positive qualities of your Moon. Rhodochrosite helps you to love yourself in a beneficial way and to express your own unique qualities out to the world.

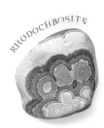
RHODOCHROSITE

This Moon demands that you explore power issues. You have to recognize your power, and own it. This does not mean having power over other people, but rather fully expressing your creative energy in the most positive way possible. One of your greatest challenges is to avoid becoming bossy. Chrysocolla reverses any destructive emotional programming you may have that drains your power. This stone supports your self-worth, and facilitates your own empowerment. Together with Citrine, it stimulates creativity at all levels.

DIOPTASE

At heart, there is something innocent and child-like about the Leo Moon and you need to express this playful side of yourself. Dioptase heals the child within, and Larimar restores your natural playfulness and joyful, child-like energy without making you behave childishly. As this stone is spiritually empowering and heals heartache, it is an excellent one to wear continuously. It will also heighten your creativity and, if you are female, connect to your innate femininity.

LARIMAR

With such a heart centred Moon, you have a pressing need to maintain, and express, an open heart. Aventurine promotes living in your own heart, and instils a sense of joy and wellbeing.

GREEN AVENTURINE

The Moon in Leo denotes a strong sexual libido. If you are not expressing this, psychosomatic dis-ease can result. Brown Opal helps to heal sexual tension that arises from an emotional cause, whilst Carnelian helps you to overcome any emotional abuse. Pink Carnelian in particular restores your trust and encourages responsiveness to your partner.

overcome **emotional blocks**

One of your strongest emotional blocks arises out of pride. Pride can keep you separated and apart, and block your heart. Your old tapes demand that you should be looked up to and admired, and anyone who transgresses this demand is frozen out. Tiger's Eye is an excellent stone for dealing with your pride. It helps you to understand the internal conflicts brought about by wilfulness and heals your self-worth. It assists in recognizing your talents, and any faults that need to be overcome. Golden (Imperial) Topaz facilitates taking pride in your own abilities while at the same time remaining open-hearted. Humility is the antidote to pride and the loving energies of Kunzite will support you in developing this quality. Apophyllite is helpful because it encourages you to abandon pretence and to be yourself, breaking down reserve and allowing your sunny nature to shine out.

If your needs are not met, or if others get all the attention, you can easily become a queen bee, around whom everything has to revolve, or a drama queen – Leo is, after all, one of the great actors of the zodiac. Carnelian is a useful stone to keep with you at all times because it ameliorates emotional tantrums and protects against envy or resentment, helping you to see the positive side of situations and supporting your love of life.

Your Moon can have mental tapes running that relate back to prejudice or bigotry instilled in childhood. Reprogramming these tapes is facilitated by placing Ametrine on your forehead for 15 minutes a day. It encourages accepting everyone with a loving heart.

nurture yourself

For you, admiration is essential sustenance. You adore being looked up to and having people think you are special. The key to self-nurturing is to discover your specialness for yourself (at the same time realizing that everyone else has their own specialness). Fuchsite is an essential stone for recognizing your own worth and value, and for releasing from the bondage of emotional power ploys.

develop your **intuition**

The expansive energy of Yellow Calcite induces a deep state of relaxation, linking to the highest source of spiritual guidance. Place it at the crown of your head to link to the universal mind, and over the third eye to open your inner eye.

YELLOW CALCITE

your leo moon **past lives**

Your Leo Moon past life roles have included the actor, ruler, despot, autocrat, dictator, bigot and benefactor. As Leo is the natural ruler of the zodiac, Leo Moon past lives tend to feature power struggles of various kinds. There has been abuse and misuse of power, and attempts to have power over others. You may have been the victim of someone else's power. Rhodochrosite provides an antidote to these lives as it insists you face the truth about yourself with loving awareness, and then heals the residue of past power ploys. You will undoubtedly have been involved in emotional games in other lives. Morganite (Pink Beryl) helps to dissolve any lasting effects, and opens your heart to unconditional love.

MORGANITE

opening the heart **ritual**

To open your heart you will need a large piece of Rose Quartz. A tumbled stone feels particularly good and polished, heart-shaped pieces are available, which make a useful reminder to keep your heart open. Hold the crystal in your hands. Close your eyes and quietly attune to the crystal. Let its loving energy flow through your hands, up your arms and into your heart. As the energy reaches your heart, feel it open and expand. Touch the crystal to your heart and absorb its healing energies, feel it gently dissolving any heartache or heartbreak. Allow your heart to fill with love. Feel your heart expanding ever outwards until the loving energy fills the whole of your body.

ROSE QUARTZ

Say out loud: 'I welcome love into my expanding heart. I am heart-centred and open to love.' Wear your Rose Quartz over your heart or place it under your pillow.

moon in virgo

MOON CRYSTAL Okenite

INTUITION CRYSTAL Kyanite

LUNAR CRYSTALS Amethyst, Azurite,

Blue Topaz, Carnelian, Charoite,

Chrysoberyl, Citrine, Fuchsite, Garnet,

Hiddenite (Green Kunzite), Jasper,

Peridot, Pietersite, Sardonyx, Smoky

Quartz, Staurolite, Violet Spinel

your moon **crystal**

OKENITE

Okenite supports the conscious manifestation of higher energies on the earth, teaching that everything is part of the cycle of the soul's lessons and that nothing has to be endured for ever. Its delicate fibres are friable so you cannot wear it – nor should you touch it – but it makes a beautiful addition to your bedside table, radiating its qualities to you as you sleep.

positive virgo **moon qualities**

BLUE TOPAZ

With the Moon in Virgo you are altruistic and caring, with enormous integrity, good sense, an excellent memory and razor-sharp perception. You combine practicality with the ability to organize and an urge to be of service. When the Moon in Virgo expresses itself positively, you connect with a deep wellspring of creative energy that finds an outlet in art or craft.

Blue Topaz is an excellent stone for you because it supports your need to be of service while at the same time taking you out of the servitude trap that leaves you always at the beck and call of others rather than discerning what is needful. While Pietersite promotes walking in your own truth.

explore your **hidden needs**

With the Moon in Virgo, one of your most powerful needs is for perfection. You constantly set high standards for yourself and other people, so much so that you are inevitably disappointed. Your high ideals mean that you often sacrifice yourself for the needs of others, and feel disappointed when others do not reciprocate. Amethyst helps you to set realistic goals and Charoite assists in accepting the present moment as already perfect. This soul stone stimulates your inner vision and helps to ground your spiritual self into everyday reality. It also encourages you on your path of spiritual service to humanity.

If you are unable to follow your deep need to be of dispassionate service, without looking for external reward or recognition, then you feel subtly dissatisfied with life. Blue Topaz is an excellent stone for you as it assists in living up to your own aspirations without reneging on your dedication to service.

Topaz insists that the scripts you live by are those you write yourself in accord with your own truth. It also teaches that true service comes from doing what is needful, and yet at the same time not allowing yourself to be put upon by others. This crystal takes you out of the servitude trap and draws the assistance of the angels of truth into your life.

Another strong Virgo Moon need is to grind things down until you reach the nub of the matter so that you understand the inner workings, and Peridot facilitates this. This stone hones your perception, and encourages you to be kinder to yourself. Most people with Virgo Moon are searching for a meaningful existence, and Sardonyx can indicate the way forward.

Driven as you are by your twin ideals of perfection and service, the Virgo Moon frequently indicates a workaholic. Staurolite is exceptionally useful for relieving stress, and negates a tendency to over-commit to your work. Azurite facilitates understanding the psychosomatic effect of the mind and emotions on the body.

Virgo is an earth sign and it may surprise you to know that you have strong sensual, rather than sexual, needs. You need to be stroked and pampered, and massage is an excellent remedy for stress.

overcome **emotional blocks**

HIDDENITE

One of the most destructive tapes that runs you is that of criticism. You criticize yourself for not living up to your exceptionally high standards, and others for failing to reach them. Encouraging you to recognize your talents and abilities, Tiger's Eye helps to release ingrained habits of criticizing yourself, while Hiddenite (Green Kunzite) gently releases feelings of failure and teaches that this is how you learn. You are also afraid of being criticized by others and Citrine makes you less sensitive to criticism, at the same time encouraging you to act on constructive criticism.

SMOKY QUARTZ

Many of your emotional blocks arise out of confusion around sex and sensuality (see Your past lives, opposite). Okenite placed by the bed releases prudishness, especially where this is linked to a past life vow of chastity, and Smoky Quartz helps to accept your physical body and your sexual nature so that passion can flow naturally.

nurture yourself

CHRYSOBERYL

You crave acknowledgement for all the small services you give to others, but are too modest to seek this out, (see Your hidden needs, page 107). This craving is often based on the need to overcome a suspicion that you are not quite good enough. Finding your own worth is nourishing for you, a task that Chrysoberyl supports, but connecting to your deep wellspring of creative energy would be more self-nurturing. Jasper, an excellent stone for self-nurturing, has the added benefit of stimulating imagination and transforming your ideas into action.

develop your **intuition**

KYANITE

Kyanite is a particularly appropriate crystal for developing your intuition because its pearly blades slice through illusion, take you into the causal level and instil spiritual integrity, a quality that your critical and rational Moon demands. You need assurance that your intuition speaks truth rather than hocus pocus, and Kyanite will provide this by linking to a spirit guide who can be trusted.

your virgo moon **past lives**

With the Moon in Virgo your past life roles have included the able administrator, the steward, the cleaner and the organizer, the health worker, the field hand or the mill owner, the haymaker and the brewer. You have experienced many service-oriented lives. These encompassed religion and the healing professions but may also have been the good and loyal servant. You may have become stuck in servitude and servility, rather than true service, and may need the assistance of Peridot to re-access your soul purpose. Fuchsite deals with issues of servitude in the past that are blocking the present life, and teaches service without false humility. If you have served out of a feeling of not being good enough, Fuchsite teaches your true worth.

Many people with strong Virgo took a vow of chastity in a past life and were taught to regard the body as sinful. This can lead to fastidiousness and difficulties with sexual expression – although there is a temptation to overcompensate for all those years of celibacy. Violet Spinel removes blockages to the rise of the kundalini force and, if your sex drive has been locked away in a past life, Carnelian placed on the lower chakras releases it. If your sex drive has gone into overdrive, then Garnet rebalances the libido (see the Releasing vows ritual, below).

releasing vows **ritual**

To release any vows or promises that no longer serve you, you will need a piece of Pietersite. Hold the crystal in your hands. Close your eyes and quietly attune to the crystal. Let its tempestuous energy flow through your body sweeping you up into a higher state of consciousness.

Say out loud:'I release all vows, promises and contracts, whether self-imposed or imposed on me by others, that no longer serve me. I let them go with love and forgiveness.' Feel the vows flowing out of your hands and into the stone.

Put down the Pietersite and bring your awareness back into your physical body, connecting to your feet and the earth. Place the Pietersite under running water for 15 minutes then wear it over your heart, or place it under your pillow at night.

moon in libra

MOON CRYSTAL Rose Quartz

INTUITION CRYSTAL Opal

LUNAR CRYSTALS Amethyst,

Aquamarine, Blue Topaz, Calcite,

Celestite, Chrysoberyl, Iolite,

Jade, Larimar, Mangano Calcite,

Rhodochrosite, Sardonyx,

Sugilite, Watermelon Tourmaline,

Wulfenite

your moon **crystal**

Rose Quartz, with its gentle, unconditional, loving energy, is an excellent stone for your relationship-oriented Moon as it purifies and opens the heart. This is the stone to use if you want to attract love, particularly as it promotes receptivity to beauty of all kinds. It also promotes the peace and harmony you crave.

positive libra **moon qualities**

SUGILITE

With the Moon in charming Libra you are courteous and well liked, and have the gifts of co-operation, diplomacy and creative compromise. Your ability to get on with everyone, and your desire for a tranquil life, can stand you in good stead, provided you avoid inauthenticity and people pleasing.

The 'love stone', Sugilite, supports relationships of all kinds, but Rose Quartz is *your* crystal because it encourages you to love yourself and attracts unconditional love into your life.

With your reputation for fairness and justice, Chrysoberyl is appropriate as it assists in forgiving and, where possible, righting injustice.

explore your **hidden needs**

You need to be needed – and to be liked. Most people with Moon in Libra only feel whole when they are in a relationship, and your challenge is to find the wholeness of your self. If you are on your own, Larimar promotes serenity and emotional equilibrium, while Celestite brings deep peace, openness to new experiences and maintains a harmonious atmosphere in times of stress. This crystal improves dysfunctional relationships by opening a space for peaceful negotiation.

Your inclination is to adapt, adjust and compromise whenever you are faced with other people's requirements, since you will do anything for a quiet life. But secretly, you want to be in control. You need your needs to be attended to. Developing willpower and strengthening your ability to assert yourself is highly beneficial and is facilitated by Sardonyx.

Another powerful Libra Moon need is for harmonious surroundings. Unless you feel that the vibes are good, you are desperately uneasy. Faced with a room full of uncongenial people, clashing colours and environmental discomfort, you feel physically ill. If you wear a calming Aquamarine, your surroundings will always feel harmonious.

overcome **emotional blocks**

One of the Libra Moon's greatest blocks is that desperate need to be in a relationship. You become lost in another person and your true feelings are submerged so that the illusion of harmony can be maintained. So often your Moon settles for second best simply to remain in a relationship. Although you are a born romantic, your old tapes run along the lines that a secure relationship is more important than true love, and that you must always please your partner. Mangano Calcite is an excellent stone for maintaining unconditional love without losing sight of yourself as an independent person.

Libra is one of the most indecisive of the signs. Your Moon sees all sides, wants to please everyone and, as a result, finds it incredibly difficult to make decisions,

WULFENITE

LAVENDER JADE

WATERMELON TOURMALINE

particularly of the emotional variety. Amethyst is an excellent stone for decision making because it combines common sense with spiritual insights, and facilitates putting them into practice.

A natural people pleaser, you could well have lost sight of your own needs and have fallen into the pattern of doing what is 'nice' rather than what is right. Your old tapes cause you to do what you have been taught is 'pleasant and acceptable'. Wulfenite stops you being sugary sweet and much too nice. By facilitating acceptance of your shadow energies, it releases you to be your authentic self. This stone is too delicate to wear and is best placed by your bed or made into an elixir that can be sipped throughout the day. (Place the crystal in a glass and stand that glass in a bowl of water in sunlight so that the vibrations can be transferred.) Iolite overcomes co-dependency with your partner, while Jade serves to encourage self-sufficiency and inner peace.

Libra has a laid-back attitude, but with the Libra Moon this can sometimes become laziness and disinclination to do anything constructive. This is particularly so when old tapes are running, but this can also be an emotional blockage. Calcite combats laziness, especially where hope or motivation has been lost.

One of your greatest fears is of facing emotional pain: yours or someone else's. At some level, you believe you will die if you have to feel such pain. This is not true, of course, but the defense you have built against such pain is strong. Watermelon Tourmaline helps you to keep your heart open and to feel the pain so that it can dissipate. At the same time, it helps you to support anyone else who is going through emotional pain.

nurture yourself

BLUE TOPAZ

Blue Topaz attunes you to your higher self. It facilitates living according to your own aspirations and views rather than living your life to please others. In paying attention to your own needs, and finding inner sources of emotional nourishment rather than feeding off a partner, you nurture yourself. In living life in an equal paternership you find inner fulfilment.

develop your **intuition**

Opal is an excellent crystal for opening your intuition. Its fine vibration enhances cosmic consciousness and mystical vision. Gazing into its iridescent depths enables you to journey into other worlds, while, at the same time, providing protection and conferring invisibility. Cherry Opal develops clairvoyance, the art of clear seeing, and clairsentience, that of clear sensing. Place it on your third eye for maximum effect.

OPAL

your libra moon **past lives**

With the Moon in Libra your past life roles include the diplomat, negotiator, marriage broker or interior designer. You may also have been the courtesan or gigolo. In many past lives you will have been 'one half of'. You have been exploring all facets of relationship and may well be caught up in karmic relationships. Larimar facilitates healing past life relationships, while Wulfenite helps you to access past life agreements with another soul, and releases you when the lesson is over. Both Wulfenite and Cerussite recognize contacts from another life. Opal shows you what your emotional state has been in other lives, and teaches you to take responsibility for your feelings. It encourages you to put out positive emotions.

CERUSSITE

attracting love **ritual**

RHODOCHROSITE

Hold a large Rhodochrosite crystal in your hands. Allow your eyes to travel along its contours, taking you on a journey into your heart. Quietly attune to the crystal, feeling its energy going out in waves. Let its gentle energy flow through your hands, up your arms and into your heart. As the energy reaches your heart, feel it open and expand. Touch the crystal to your heart and welcome its soothing vibration. Allow your heart to be purified by the crystal, feel any old pain or abuse dissolve as its warm, unconditional love fills your heart and spills out through your whole body. Say, out loud: 'I welcome love into my heart and into my life. I am a magnet for love.' Sit quietly for a few moments. When you have finished, place the crystal by your bed.

m moon in scorpio

MOON CRYSTAL Smoky Quartz

INTUITION CRYSTAL Herkimer Diamond

LUNAR CRYSTALS Agate, Apache Tear, Beryl, Black Obsidian, Charoite, Dioptase, Green Jasper, Hawk's Eye, Herkimer Diamond, Labradorite, Malachite, Rhodochrosite, Rhodonite, Rutilated Quartz (Angel Hair), Sceptre Quartz, Smithsonite, Turquoise

your moon **crystal**

SMOKY QUARTZ

Smoky Quartz is an essential crystal for your emotionally intense Moon as it promotes detoxification and elimination on all levels, teaching you how to leave behind everything that no longer serves you. It fortifies your resolve and gives you strength during difficult times, enabling you to face these with equanimity.

positive **moon qualities**

RUTILATED QUARTZ

With the Moon in Scorpio you have enormous perspicacity, the knowledge that you will survive no matter what, and a tremendous capacity for self-transformation. This makes you an excellent guide for people who are exploring the dark places with which you are so familiar, and your ability to see below the surface also makes you an effective healer.

Rutilated Quartz (Angel Hair) is a wonderful support for your soul, it brings out the positive qualities of your Moon, while Hawk's Eye helps you to change your focus and soar above the world rather than dwelling in the depths.

explore your **hidden needs**

Your need is for emotional intensity and strong commitment. Anything less makes you feel insecure. This Moon sign holds on to the past and to entrenched emotions such as resentment or jealousy, so you have a powerful need for emotional release as there will have been traumas in your past. Your needs tend to be compulsive and forceful, erupting from the depths of your subconscious mind. This is a cathartic Moon that takes many trips down into the places other people fear to tread. Indeed, exploring all the taboo areas of life is one of your greatest needs. Facing your own darkness transforms your experiences into fertile compost for new growth and this is facilitated by Smoky Quartz. Place a Smoky Quartz point-down below your feet to draw off negative energies, and hold one to facilitate the insights that will set you free from the tyranny of your dark emotions.

HAWK'S EYE

Just as you need to explore the depths of darkness, so too you can rise to experience the heights of consciousness. To facilitate initiation into the mysteries, wear Labradorite. This is a highly protective and mystical stone, a bringer of light. It raises your consciousness, removes psychic debris and transforms your awareness.

LABRADORITE

overcome **emotional blocks**

The Scorpio Moon has some of the most toxic old tapes and the most entrenched emotional blocks, but the good news is that these can be transformed. Resentment, power struggles, fear of inadequacy or abandonment, alienation and ancient rejection are just some of the poisonous residues that could be unconsciously motivating your behaviour.

SMITHSONITE

Bitterness of the heart can be healed with Agate. This stone releases inner anger and emotional trauma, fosters love and creates security by dissolving internal tension. If you are disheartened after trauma, Agate promotes trying again. Lavender-Pink Smithsonite heals past experiences of abandonment and abuse, rebuilding trust and security, while Green Agate encourages emotional flexibility. Fire Agate dissolves your destructive desires, Moss Agate helps you to shed your emotional baggage and

MOSS AGATE

Dioptase heals betrayal and the pain of abandonment. Green Jasper helps you to release from obsessions and compulsions. It restores balance when one part of your life has become all important to the detriment of others.

GREEN JASPER

nurture yourself

Intensity and all-consuming passion provide nourishment for you. When you are emotionally fed and sexually fulfilled, you are empowered. When you suffer emotional deprivation, you retreat into abusive power over others. Self-nurturing is facilitated by drawing emotional nourishment from your own inner reserves rather than demanding it from others. Charoite, the stone of transformation, is excellent for promoting self-nurturing. It overcomes your resistance, provides deep emotional healing and puts things into perspective. This is an excellent stone for conquering the compulsions and obsessions of your alienated Moon, and for releasing frustration at all levels.

CHAROITE

develop your intuition

HERKIMER DIAMOND

A Herkimer Diamond resonates with your own sharp perception. In its smaller, clear form it is excellent for opening the third eye and for connecting to the highest spiritual levels. It has a crystal memory into which information can be poured for later retrieval. In its larger form, it creates a protective grid around you. Two Herkimer Diamonds can be programmed to enhance telepathy between partners.

your scorpio moon past lives

BLACK OBSIDIAN

Past life roles for the Scorpio Moon tend to be associated with alchemy, medicine, death and anything clandestine. Your previous lives have centred around power and exploring the great mysteries of life, and you may well have experienced persecution and trauma. You have been the priest and the healer, the midwife and, quite possibly, the death-bringer, as you explored all that was hidden and forbidden. Black Obsidian addresses previous misuse of power. It composts the past to facilitate soul growth, helping release negative energies, while Rhodochrosite assists in healing the past and shows you the gift in your experiences. Hawk's Eye brings to the surface emotions or dis-ease from previous lives, and Turquoise teaches you that karma is ongoing and that you are the creator of your own reality.

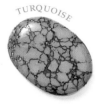

Sceptre Quartz is a naturally formed crystal point wrapped around the end of a rod that looks rather like a crystal phallus. This occult symbol of power puts you in touch with esoteric abilities from another life, and is a powerful healing tool for karmic dis-ease, especially if misuse of sexual power has been involved. Malachite is useful for psycho-sexual problems that stem from past life causes because it unlocks the reason behind the dis-ease. Malachite may need to be tempered with the compassionate, forgiving energies of Rhodochrosite. Dioptase teaches you that pain and difficulty in a relationship stem from inner separation from your self. This powerful heart healer repairs that link and fills the emotional black hole that is desperate for love. It releases the considerable wisdom you have acquired in past lives.

forgiveness **ritual**

To give and receive forgiveness, you will need a large piece of Rhodonite. Hold the crystal in your hands. Allow your eyes to travel over its surface. You will notice that it combines red with black, showing you both sides of an issue. Close your eyes and quietly attune to the crystal. Let its vibrant energy flow through your hands, up your arms and into your heart. As the energy reaches your heart, feel it open and expand. Touch the crystal to your heart and think of the person or situation that needs forgiveness. Allow the Rhodonite to absorb any resentment you may be holding and feel its forgiving energy enter your heart and flow through your whole body.

Say, out loud: 'I welcome forgiveness into my heart and into my life. I forgive all those who have caused me hurt and ask forgiveness from those I have wronged.' Sit quietly for a few moments with your eyes focused on the crystal. When you have finished, place the crystal under running water for 15 minutes to cleanse it. Then wear it, or place it under your pillow.

moon in sagittarius

MOON CRYSTAL Apophyllite

INTUITION CRYSTAL Lapis Lazuli

LUNAR CRYSTALS Azurite,

Blue Lace Agate, Cerussite, Charoite,

Emerald, Garnet, Lapis Lazuli, Lepidolite,

Moss Agate, Nebula Stone, Okenite,

Rhodochrosite, Rhyolite, Sodalite,

Topaz, Wulfenite

your moon **crystal**

The Stone of Truth, Apophyllite encourages you to be introspective and to recognize your true self. It also has the additional benefit of making you feel more comfortable within your physical body. This stone carries an esoteric record of all that has happened on earth and brings forward knowledge from the past and the future. Use it as a bridge between the physical and spiritual worlds and to facilitate journeys out of the body.

positive sagittarius **moon qualities**

This is an entertaining, companionable and optimistic Moon with a fund of wisdom to draw on. Nevertheless, your independent Moon speaks your mind, and some other signs find it difficult to face your relentless honesty, but when this is tempered with kindness it can provide powerful insights.

Topaz keeps you connected to your inner wisdom and to your feelings so that you can make these work for you. Your Sagittarius Moon has in the past learned how to detach from emotions and Blue Lace Agate is an excellent stone for reconnecting to your emotions without being overwhelmed by them.

explore your **hidden needs**

You are driven by a need for emotional freedom. Your restless Moon wants space to explore and be itself, particularly in relationships. If your partner is able to grant this space, then you will probably return. If not, you will move on to the next relationship. Garnet is an excellent stone for encouraging commitment, while leaving space within the relationship to be yourself, and Charoite helps you to live in the present moment rather than in future potentials. This stone also assists in finding the gift in all that you encounter.

RED GARNET

Truth is another powerful need, and you instinctively know when you are being lied to. Your quest for knowledge never ceases and Lapis Lazuli is useful because it leads to inner truth while linking you to universal truth. Your philosophical Moon has explored many avenues and pulling your knowledge into practice is essential. This is facilitated by Wulfenite.

CHAROITE

Expressing your feelings is something you find difficult but, to fully be yourself, this is essential. Blue Lace Agate helps you to safely express both your thoughts and your feelings, and Cerussite teaches you how to be tactful in any situation – an enormous challenge for your outspoken Moon.

overcome **emotional blocks**

EMERALD

You act impulsively on instinct, and then regret your actions. Jasper encourages you to think before acting, while Lepidolite helps to reprogramme your behaviour. Emerald teaches infinite patience and this stone can help you to wait until you can see the way ahead before making a move. While you are happy to discuss feelings, you may well use words to create an emotional block rather than actually feel the feelings. Moss Agate is an excellent stone for dissolving repressed feelings and bringing them gently to the surface for your acceptance.

LEPIDOLITE

With a Sagittarius Moon you tend to believe that the grass is greener somewhere else. Emotional commitment is difficult, and you dislike emotional demands and any form of neediness, which means that you move on rather than deal with issues, forever chasing your dream. Okenite anchors you into a more stable way of life and helps to deal with the dualities within your own nature.

nurture yourself

Topaz sheds light on your pathway and helps to tap into your inner resources and cosmic wisdom. This stone promotes honesty and openness. Bringing abundant joy, generosity and good health, it is an excellent emotional support that makes you receptive to love from every source. Discovering true intimacy is highly beneficial and wearing Topaz nurtures you at every level. If you use your innate honesty and trust within a relationship, shared feelings will bring you joy.

develop your intuition

The deep blue of Lapis Lazuli is the key to spiritual attainment. It takes you effortlessly into the highest levels of spiritual awareness to contact spirit guardians. This beautiful stone opens your third eye and enhances your spiritual vision. It ensures that you always speak the truth. Place it by your bed for intuitive dream work and on your third eye to promote clear seeing.

your sagittarius moon past lives

In your past lives you will have been the teacher and the priest, the mentor and the explorer, the quester and questioner, as you sought out knowledge wherever it could be found. You may well have confused religion with spirituality and your challenge now is to reconnect to the spirit, for which Azurite is a potent tool. In your desire for a just world, you may also have fought for freedom and independence. In the process, you may have become stuck in belief patterns that no longer serve you. Sodalite releases these, but you may also have considerable karmic wisdom, which Rhyolite can help you to access. This stone processes the past and integrates it with the present, bringing things to resolution and encouraging you to move forward. If you fell into the trap of telling people what to believe, rather than being an example to them, then Azurite releases your inspirational qualities.

Unfortunately, Sagittarius may also have been the liar, the thief or the conman who lived off his wits. If there is reparation to be made, Rhodonite will assist you (see the Forgiveness ritual, page 117) while Apophyllite, the Stone of Truth, re-establishes your integrity.

RHODONITE

the grail **ritual**

At its deepest level, Sagittarius is on a quest for the grail within. The grail is the point of stillness around which everything else revolves. A place where there is nothing to do, one simply has to be. To learn the secret of being, and to find the inner grail, you will need a Nebula Stone.

SODALITE

Hold the Nebula Stone in your hands and close your eyes. Feel the vibration of light held within the stone travelling into your hands and into every cell of your being. Allow this vibration to activate the cells of your physical body to a higher state of awareness.

Now feel the vibration of light moving slowly out through the different levels of your being from the physical to the emotional, the mental to the karmic, until it reaches the spiritual. Be aware that you are a spiritual being who is on a human journey. Feel the immense age of your soul and become aware of the enormous potential within your being.

NEBULA STONE

Open your eyes and gaze into the Nebula Stone's depths. It will take you out into infinity and inward into the smallest particle of being. As you gaze with unfocused eyes, the two become one. This is a stone of non-duality. Allow it to take you into a space of timeless oneness, into the grail within. Enjoy simply being, knowing that there is nothing to do, but everything to allow.

When you are ready, return your attention to the room, be aware of your feet firmly on the floor and of settling into your physical body. Keep your Nebula Stone where you can see it to remind you to *be*.

moon in capricorn

MOON CRYSTAL Snow Quartz

INTUITION CRYSTAL Phantom Quartz

LUNAR CRYSTALS Ametrine, Aquamarine, Blue Lace Agate, Calcite, Charoite, Chrysanthemum Stone, Galena, Garnet, Iron Pyrite, Magnesite, Moonstone, Pietersite, Pyrolusite, Rhodochrosite, Serpentine

your moon **crystal**

Snow Quartz provides you with rock-solid support and encourages you to let go of your burdens and baggage so that you can attune to your deep inner wisdom. This stone gently supports you while you fulfil necessary duties and obligations, but it also points out where you are yourself creating responsibilities that indirectly help you to feel needed, or which inflate your self-importance in an attempt to overcome any feelings of inadequacy.

positive capricorn **moon qualities**

With your Moon in Capricorn you are a diligent, responsible person whose urge is towards doing what is right and to being useful to society. Although cautious, you have an innate authority. This can mean that you care deeply about people and work for their best interests, but it may indicate that you seek to control your environment. In a relationship, you are solid and dependable, with a deep commitment to your partner, qualities that are encouraged by wearing Garnet. When this Moon is working positively, it can create an urge towards the spiritual side of life.

explore your **hidden needs**

Your Moon often feels cut off and unloved, and unable to express feelings. People with a Capricorn Moon tend to repress and sublimate their emotional needs into material things, or into reaching the top, and yet, you long for deep emotional connection with others. Magnesite helps you to love yourself, an essential preliminary to accepting love from other people. Iron Pyrite assists in overcoming feelings of inadequacy and imparts confidence. Helpful if you have an inferiority complex, this stone is particularly useful for men who feel inferior as it strengthens confidence in yourself and your masculinity. This stone overcomes the melancholy and deep despair to which Capricorn Moon is prone.

IRON PYRITE

Many Capricorn Moon men feel cut off from the feminine, intuitive side of their nature, and yet are aware of a need to reconnect to this. Moonstone is filled with receptive, passive, feminine energy that facilitates this contact. It is the perfect antidote for a macho man or an aggressive female.

MOONSTONE

overcome **emotional blocks**

Tightly controlled and emotionally cool, Capricorn is the Moon of 'oughts' and 'shoulds'. So many of your old tapes are concerned with what you ought to do, or what you should be thinking or believing. Your Moon has internalized all the authoritarian voices from your past and you need to release these and tune into the voice of your own self (see the Inner voice ritual, page 125).

CHAROITE

Most of your emotional blockages are concerned with the repression of feelings and the fear of being judged. Your childhood was most probably somewhat lacking in affection or warmth and, as a result, emotionally stultifying, and you would have been approved of only if you conformed to family expectations. You then became emotionally controlled and now find it very difficult to express your feelings. Blue Lace Agate dissolves emotional repression from whatever cause, and overcomes coldness and rejection. If your negative emotional programming and expectations have induced a pessimistic approach to life, Ametrine can assist. If you are driven by

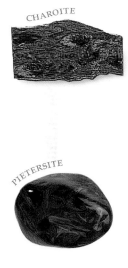

PIETERSITE

other people's programmes, Charoite is the stone for you, while Pietersite releases from other people's authoritarianism. Green Calcite is an excellent stone for removing rigid beliefs and old programmes. If you have yourself become judgemental, Aquamarine makes you more tolerant. This stone is particularly helpful because it gives support when you feel overwhelmed by responsibility and it removes self-defeating programmes. Use this stone to encourage a personality that is upright, persistent and dynamic.

If you find that your emotional blocks include bigotry, narrow-mindedness or self-righteousness, then Chrysanthemum Stone removes these. Snow Quartz helps to let go of overwhelming responsibilities and limitations, and Sunstone turns even the most incorrigible pessimist into an optimist, switching to a positive take on matters. This sunny stone can lift the darkest mood and it is excellent for removing inhibitions and hang-ups.

nurture yourself

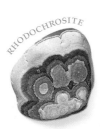

You crave approval and seek emotional control but loving yourself is the most effective way to self-nurture, and this is facilitated by the gentle energies of Rhodochrosite. If you are repelled by this stone, it is an indication that you are repressing something you need to look at. Rhodochrosite draws out and dissolves the problem, increasing your self-worth.

develop your intuition

Phantom Quartz symbolizes universal awareness and this ghostly stone stimulates the ability to read from the Akashic Record – the spiritual record of everything that has, and will, be. If you want to access the plan for your present life, or to evaluate your spiritual progress, choose an Amethyst Phantom, and if self-realization is your aim, then choose a Green Chlorite Phantom. A Smoky Phantom links into the purpose of a group incarnation, attracting members of your soul group, and stimulating purity of intention.

your capricorn moon **past lives**

Your past life roles will have included the judge and the lawyer, the policer of society's rules, the administrator and record keeper, and the astute businessperson but you could also have been the domestic drudge keeping order in the home. You may have been the pastor, or the inheritor of property and status. It is likely that you have been in the highest echelons of power but that lack of belief in your self may also have held you back. Galena takes you beyond self-limiting assumptions from the past and Pyrolusite releases the influence of authority figures. No matter what your past life role has been, there is an inheritance of karmic wisdom that can be accessed with the help of Serpentine. This earthing stone also puts you in control of your life – a comfortable place for Capricorn.

GALENA

SERPENTINE

inner voice **ritual**

To connect to your own inner voice, rather than those of external authorities, you will need a piece of Pyrolusite. Hold the crystal in your hands. Allow your softly focused eyes to wander over its surface and quietly attune to its delicate, fan-like matrix. Let the matrix transport you into the depths of yourself. Feel it dissolving the mental influence of others, setting you free from emotional manipulation, and releasing all the beliefs that have been imposed from outside yourself. Feel a connection opening to the voice of your inner self, and welcome the guidance that is there for you.

PYROLUSITE

Say out loud: 'I stay true to my own beliefs and follow my own pathway. I listen to the inner voice of my self and use that as my guide. I am open to its signals however they may present.' Wait quietly, listening for the inner voice and being aware of any subtle signals it may use to contact you.

Keep the Pyrolusite close beside you and hold it whenever the counsel of your inner voice is required.

moon in aquarius

MOON CRYSTAL Clear Quartz

INTUITION CRYSTAL Aquamarine

LUNAR CRYSTALS Aquamarine, Beryl, Boji Stones, Celestite, Cerussite, Chalcedony, Charoite, Chiastolite, Chrysoprase, Gold-Sheen Obsidian, Moldavite, Rhodonite, Rose Quartz, Selenite, Soulmate Crystal, Sulphur, Vanadinite

your moon **crystal**

Clear Quartz has a very clear vibration. It absorbs, stores, releases and regulates energy and makes you feel less wired as it discharges the build up of static energy that accumulates within your physical body. Quartz is piezoelectric, that is to say it gives off sparks of energy and light that resonate with the electrical circuits in your brain, harmonizing them to a new vibration that supports your evolution on all levels. This lively crystal overcomes your paradoxical but deep-seated fear of change.

positive aquarius **moon qualities**

With your Moon in Aquarius you are original, eccentric and independent, with a flair for science. You are deeply concerned about the future of humanity and of the planet, and you have enormous potential for expressing universal love. You can look forward into the future to see what will be needed for the good of everyone, and you have the ability to be emotionally objective, unswayed by arguments that tug at the heartstrings. Your desire to facilitate social change and the evolution of humankind is strengthened by the delicate vibrations of Blue Celestite.

explore your **hidden needs**

You have a strong need for emotional independence and yet can feel cut off and isolated from the rest of humanity. Chalcedony enhances brotherhood and a soulmate crystal (two same-sized crystals naturally joined together along one side) can help to find the intimacy you need in relationships of all kinds. Even when you have developed intimacy, there will still be times when you need emotional space and freedom. Garnet is an excellent stone for promoting the kind of commitment that allows the space to be yourself. Give one to your partner to enhance trust in your ability to return to closeness when you are ready.

BLUE CHALCEDONY

Many people with Aquarius Moon feel as though they do not belong to earth. Cerussite helps to recognize why you chose to come to earth, the tasks you have to do and the gifts you bring to advance the evolution of humanity.

People with Aquarius Moon yearn both to be fully accepted and to be reunited with their true home. Moldavite eases this homesickness. It can be used for extraterrestrial contact and for accessing cosmic messengers. Charoite overcomes feelings of alienation and brings deep soul healing, while Rhodonite welcomes you into the brotherhood of humanity.

SOULMATE

overcome **emotional blocks**

Aloofness and a desire for independence can lead to alienation, loneliness and erratic behaviour, which needs to be brought under your conscious control. You are running a powerful tape that centres around rebellion and change. There is a part of you that wants change for change's sake, and another part that is deeply fixed and which resists change at all costs. As a result, your emotions swing wildly. Selenite stabilizes erratic emotions and disperses the cause; this spiritually oriented stone can be the catalyst for spiritual growth. Aquamarine is particularly useful for understanding the emotional states that underlie your resistance to change. It is helpful if you need emotional closure since it promotes courage and encourages taking responsibility for oneself.

SELENITE

AQUAMARINE

ROSE QUARTZ

If you are stuck in an old pattern of rebellion and wilfulness, Sulphur can assist. It softens that part of your personality that tends automatically to do the opposite of whatever is suggested, and which never obeys instructions.

A self-contained soul, you find it difficult to relate on a one-to-one basis and commitment is even more problematic for you – indeed, you may well be commitment-phobic. When challenged by relationships you retreat into a cold and lonely place. If someone comes close, you back away because you have a deep fear of intimacy. Rose Quartz can heal your fears and help you to find deep intimacy and closeness in relationships.

GREEN CHIASTOLITE

With two such different ruling planets, controlling Saturn and unpredictable Uranus, you often feel torn apart. It is rather like driving a car flat out with the brakes fully on. Chiastolite helps to stabilize you and overcome the fear of going mad that the chaotic and unstable Uranus can impart.

nurture yourself

VANADINITE

Vanadinite is an excellent stone for bringing you fully into incarnation. It gently grounds your spirit into the physical body and helps you to be comfortable in the earth environment, while maintaining a strong connection with universal energy. Daily meditation, together with the knowledge that you are a spiritual being who is presently on a human journey, is an excellent way to self-nurture.

develop your intuition

AQUAMARINE

Aquamarine is a wonderful stone for meditation as it quietens the mind and facilitates obtaining communication from the higher planes. Clearing extraneous thoughts, it invokes a high state of consciousness and spiritual awareness, and encourages dispassionate service to humanity. If the spiritual and physical bodies have become misaligned, Aquamarine gently realigns them, releasing intuitive communication on all levels. Placed on the third eye, Aquamarine promotes clairvoyance and sharpens your intuition.

your aquarius moon **past lives**

With the Moon in Aquarius your past life roles would have been revolutionary, world-changing, freedom-loving and non-conformist, but you could equally well be the maker of rules and imposer of regulations. Your previous lives were concerned with change and evolution as you struggled to bring in new ideas and overturn the status quo. You could well have been the outcast or the scapegoat.

ANGELITE

Upheavals of all kinds feature in your past. You are aware that the earth is not as stable as it appears because it is not uncommon for people with strong Aquarius influences to have been buried by an erupting volcano or pounded by an earthquake. You also know that society can erupt at any time. If you have *déjà vu* or recurrent nightmares, these could well have a past life cause. Sleeping with Chrysoprase under your pillow releases these images from your mind and ensures a good night's sleep. If you were in any way brainwashed, Boji Stones assist in removing mental imprints and hypnotic commands, putting you back in control of your mind. These stones also help you to ground yourself into the earth's vibration. Angelite facilitates speaking your truth, no matter how way-out that may be, and it assists you in being more compassionate and tolerant, especially of what cannot be changed.

CHRYSOPRASE

scrying **ritual**

Before commencing, make sure you will not be disturbed. Take your crystal ball into your hands. Hold it for a few moments to attune to your energy. If you have a specific question, focus on this as you do so. Now place the ball on a stand or cloth in front of you. Allow your eyes to soften and your intuition to come into focus. Look obliquely at the ball. Let your vision wander into its depths. Keep your eyes relaxed. Images may appear within the ball or in your mind's eye. You may become aware of feelings in your body or 'hear' thoughts dropping into your mind. Do not try to interpret at this stage, simply observe. Write down what you see, even if it appears to be meaningless. You will quickly learn to interpret images as your intuition develops. When you have completed your scrying, cleanse the ball, then cover it.

CRYSTAL BALL

♓ moon in pisces

MOON CRYSTAL Amethyst

INTUITION CRYSTAL Celestite

LUNAR CRYSTALS Angelite,
Aventurine, Blue Lace Agate, Boji Stones,
Celestite, Chiastolite, Chrysoprase,
Cymophane, Danburite, Fire Agate,
Fluorite, Fuchsite, Jasper, Kunzite,
Magnesite, Morganite (Pink Beryl), Opal
Aura Quartz, Rhodochrosite, Ruby in
Zoisite (Anyolite), Selenite, Sunstone,
Tiger's Eye

your moon **crystal**

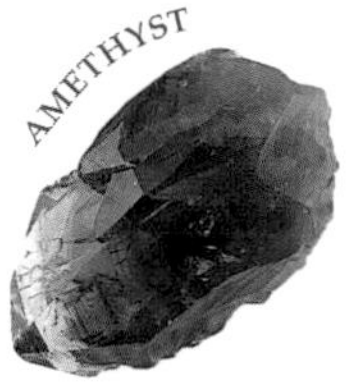

Amethyst is a wonderfully protective and cleansing crystal that brings you tranquillity and peace. It encourages you to develop common sense and to become more emotionally centred and focused.

positive pisces **moon qualities**

With the Moon in receptive Pisces you are a deeply caring and empathic person who has the ability to move between everyday consciousness and spiritual awareness – although you need to be aware of a tendency to gullibility. Your strongly developed intuition gives you enormous psychic gifts. Amethyst is an excellent stone for you as it focuses your vision and enhances your love of the divine. You tend to confuse pity with love, and sympathy with empathy, but if you develop your capacity for deep emotional sharing you can be of enormous help to other people. Aventurine is an excellent stone for promoting your compassion.

explore your **hidden needs**

One of your most powerful needs is to be needed. You experience yourself through emotional interaction with other people, and receive your emotional satisfaction through 'helping'.

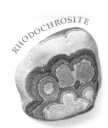

RHODOCHROSITE

Your Moon is highly sensitive and real life is a little too harsh for you so you seek solace in fantasy – or a bottle (see Emotional blocks, below). You long for self-immolation within the divine, or union with another soul. This is a symbiotic Moon and you seek an emotionally melded partnership. Searching for the perfect relationship, you often settle for less, but find it difficult to separate from previous lovers (see the Tie cutting ritual, page 101). Rhodochrosite promotes selfless love and compassion, Cymophane links into unconditional love, while Celestite and Chrysoprase bring about a strong connection to the divine. Ruby in Zoisite promotes your individuality while retaining interconnectedness with the rest of humanity.

CHRYSOPRASE

You are subject to overwhelming needs as your emotions are powerful currents that pull you this way and that without thought or reason. Lacking boundaries you are acutely aware of other people's pain, and are invaded by their thoughts and feelings. Fluorite helps to discern when outside influences are at work within yourself and shuts off psychic manipulation and undue mental influence. This protective stone makes you more aware of spiritual realities. Constructing strong boundaries for yourself is important and Kunzite imparts the ability to be self-contained, even in a crowd, as it strengthens the subtle energy fields around your body.

RUBY WITH ZOISITE

overcome **emotional blocks**

MORGANITE (PINK BERYL)

Your strongest tapes centre around victim-martyr-saviour-rescuer (see Your past lives, see page 132) and the delusions and deceptions that accompany this – although there may well be karma around white lies. Given your tendency to self-sacrifice and self-immolation, Morganite (Pink Beryl) is useful as it clears victim mentality and prevents you taking on the suffering of others. You have difficulty saying 'no' and make sacrifices for others, and Sunstone removes these tendencies.

FIRE AGATE

This is the escapist Moon and you may well find yourself caught up in addictions or compulsions of all kinds. Fire Agate is excellent for alleviating cravings and addictions. Guilt, your strongest emotional blockage, is an underlying cause of addiction; it is alleviated with the assistance of Chiastolite. Jasper encourages you to be honest with yourself, drawing your attention to any self-deception, and Gold Tiger's Eye helps to make decisions from a place of reason rather than emotion. Boji Stones hold you gently in incarnation, and dissolve blockages in the subtle bodies that surround your physical body. Blue Lace Agate is particularly useful for helping Pisces Moon men to accept their extreme sensitivity and emotionality.

BOJI STONES

nurture yourself

People with a strong Pisces Moon tend to feed off other people, especially through a strong emotional bond. What would genuinely nurture you is union with your divine self and this is promoted by meditating with Opal Aura Quartz.

ANGELITE

develop your **intuition**

The ethereal blue crystals of Celestite are imbued with divine energies that impel you towards enlightenment and union with the divine. This beautiful stone has the power to contact angels, particularly in its compacted form, Angelite. It stimulates clairvoyant communication, aids dream recall and teaches trust in the wisdom of the divine. This stone holds the vision of total harmony and peaceful co-existence for the whole of creation.

BLUE CELESTITE

your pisces moon **past lives**

With the Moon in Pisces your past life roles could well have been that of the sailor, the fisherman and the mystic. You have had many religious lives and ones closely connected with the sea. An artist at heart, you could well have been a poet. Pisces Moon previous lives strongly feature the victim-martyr-saviour-syndrome.

Confusing pity with love and wanting to atone, you desired to take on the suffering of others in a positive way, but the reality was more often the martyr or the victim. Fuchsite is excellent for dealing with many aspects of your past. It is essential for those who automatically move into saviour or rescuer mode and then quickly become victims. Combating repeating patterns of dependence and co-dependence, Fuchsite releases both souls to their own pathway. Selenite accesses the plan for the present life and pinpoints lessons still being worked on, showing how they can be resolved.

unconditional love **ritual**

To access unconditional love you will need a piece of ethereal Danburite. Hold the crystal in your hands and allow your eyes to travel into its brilliant depths. This stone takes you on a journey through the celestial realms. Close your eyes and quietly attune to the crystal, feeling its energy lifting you to the highest possible vibration. Let this pure vibration flow through your hands, up your arms, into your heart and then up into the higher heart chakra, just above the heart. Be aware that cosmic light is flooding into your higher heart chakra. As the energy reaches your higher heart chakra, place the Danburite over it, feel the chakra open and expand. With this cosmic light comes the serenity of unconditional love. Bathe yourself in this love.

Say, to yourself: 'I welcome spiritual love into my heart and into my life. I reach out to the angels and to all higher beings, and ask that I will be opened to unconditional love and eternal wisdom.'

When you have finished the ritual, bring your attention back into your physical body. Be aware of your feet on the floor and your connection to the earth. Allow unconditional love to flow into the earth so that it may be carried to wherever it is needed. Take a deep breath, bring your attention firmly back into the room, then get up and move around. Wrap the Danburite safely and place it under your pillow. Meditate with it daily.

THE CRYSTAL ZODIAC MANDALA

capricorn

sagittarius

aquarius

scorpio

pisces

libra

aries

virgo

taurus

leo

gemini

cancer

career, social status, outer environment, old age

religion and ethics, higher education, long journeys, philosophy

friendship, society, social awareness, group activities

sex, birth–death–rebirth, inherited resources, occult

mysticism, escapism, secrets, spiritual yearnings

marriage, relationship, partnership, adulthood

individuality, personality, appearance, childhood

health, service, vocation, teamwork

values, personal resources, possessions, self-worth

creativity, self-expression, children, love affairs

education, communication, siblings, short journeys

home, parents, inherited patterns, inner environment

The crystal zodiac mandala takes your understanding of astrology and birthstones a giant step forward. The wheel (opposite) shows you which signs are associated with which particular facet of life and you can use this to fill in under-strength or missing areas of your life. The mandala can also attune you to unfolding energies within your birthchart: progression is a tool with which astrologers symbolically mature the chart to reflect how your life is developing and changing, and you can do this yourself (see page 137). If you understand astrology, you can also use the mandala to attune to the effects of transits to your chart.

making the mandala

* Starting with Aries, take a few moments to attune to the birthstones and sign – you may like to read the description of the birthstones for the signs (see pages 8–57) before placing them on the wheel.
* Move on to Taurus and repeat the process, and then each sign of the zodiac in turn.
* When all the stones have been laid out, with your eyes half closed, contemplate the whole wheel. Notice which colours or stones attract your attention, be aware which parts of the wheel seem more remote or hidden. Keep your attention focused on the wheel until it looks evenly balanced. If necessary, pick up an out-of-balance birthstone and hold it for a few moments until the energies resonate with you.
* When you have finished the meditation, remove the stones in the reverse order and place them in a bag for safekeeping.

using crystals with your birthchart

You can take the crystal zodiac mandala a stage further by placing crystals linked to the planets on your birthchart (see page 136). Hold the appropriate stone for a few moments before placing it over the glyph for the planet. When the placement is complete, spend 15 minutes quietly contemplating the whole chart. The beneficial effect is enhanced by placing a photograph of yourself in the centre of the chart and leaving the stones in place for several days.

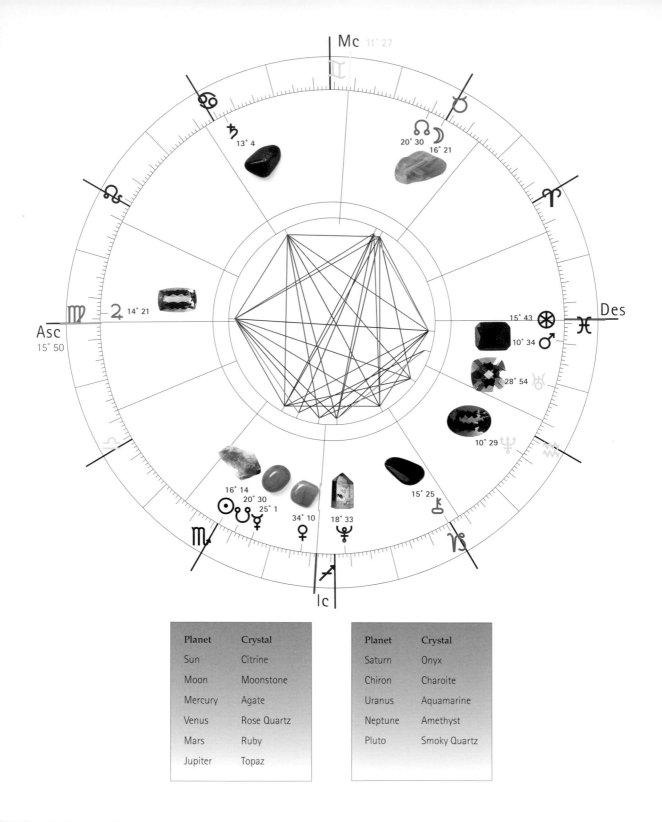

Mc 11° 27

Des

Asc 15° 50

Ic

13° 4

20° 30 16° 21

2 14° 21

15° 43
10° 34

28° 54

10° 29

16° 14
20° 30
25° 1

34° 10

18° 33

15° 25

Planet	Crystal
Sun	Citrine
Moon	Moonstone
Mercury	Agate
Venus	Rose Quartz
Mars	Ruby
Jupiter	Topaz

Planet	Crystal
Saturn	Onyx
Chiron	Charoite
Uranus	Aquamarine
Neptune	Amethyst
Pluto	Smoky Quartz

the unfolding birthchart

The birthchart does not remain static; it unfolds and develops throughout your life. Even if you know nothing about astrology, you can attune to this developmental cycle – which is called the progressed chart. Progression is based on the symbolic movement of the planets in which one day equals a year. If you have astrological knowledge, or have had your birthchart read by an astrologer, you will know the progressed placements of your planets and can lay out the stones for the progressed chart as you did for your birthchart. This is a very potent process as it aligns you with all the changes taking place in your inner psyche.

If you have no astrological knowledge, you can align yourself with the process by moving on to the crystals for the signs into which your Sun, Moon or Ascendant has moved. The Sun and the Ascendant take around 30 years to move through a sign, symbolically moving one degree a year. If you were born during the first ten days of a birth sign, your Sun is at the beginning of the sign and will take between 20 and 30 years to symbolically progress to the next sign, so you will be between 20 and 30 years of age when the birthstone for the next sign becomes appropriate. If you were born in the middle ten days of a sign, it will take between ten and 20 years to change signs, and if you were born in the last ten days, it will have changed signs by the time you are ten years of age. After this, the Sun will change signs approximately every 30 years.

To ascertain your progressed Moon, add your age to the day of your birth and find the Moon placement for the new date in your birth year in the tables on pages 140–141. If you are now 35, for example, and were born on 17 October, you would add 35 to 17. Making allowances for there being 31 days in October, this would give you a progressed Moon date of 21 November in the year of your birth.

You can also lay out your birthchart with appropriate stones for planetary transits around the outside of your birthchart. Quietly meditating with the chart will bring the unfolding energies more directly into your awareness.

APPENDIX

Zodiac signs

♈ Aries

♉ Taurus

♊ Gemini

♋ Cancer

♌ Leo

♍ Virgo

♎ Libra

♏ Scorpio

♐ Sagittarius

♑ Capricorn

♒ Aquarius

♓ Pisces

astrological time

Astrological calculations are based on Greenwich Mean Time so you need to make adjustments for the time and place you were born, and for any Daylight Saving or Summer Time. Places east of London have the time difference subtracted from Local Time to give GMT, and places west of London have the time difference added to Local Time to give GMT.

finding your ascendant

* Using the ascendant tables opposite, select the latitude closest to that of your birthplace.
* Lay a ruler across the table. Swivel the ruler so that the top edge aligns on the right-hand side with your time of birth (allowing for Daylight Saving if applicable).
* Adjust the ruler to line up with your day of birth.
* The sign that the ruler passes through is your most probable Ascendant. For example, a birthplace of latitude 51° 32' N, with a time of birth of 1.30 am on 20 March, gives a Sagittarius Ascendant.

finding your moon sign

* Using the Moon Tables on pages 140–141, find the position of the Moon on day one of your birth month and year.
* Using the Days of the Moon table on page 140, find your day of birth. Read off how many signs or degrees to count forward from the first day of the month position (there are 30 degrees in a sign). This gives a rough guide. If the Moon is close to the beginning or end of a sign, your Moon may be the preceding or following sign. For example, if the position of the moon on day one of your birth month and year is 24 degrees Gemini, and 20 is your day of birth, you should count forward 9 signs from Gemini, which gives you a Moon sign of Pisces.

ascendant tables

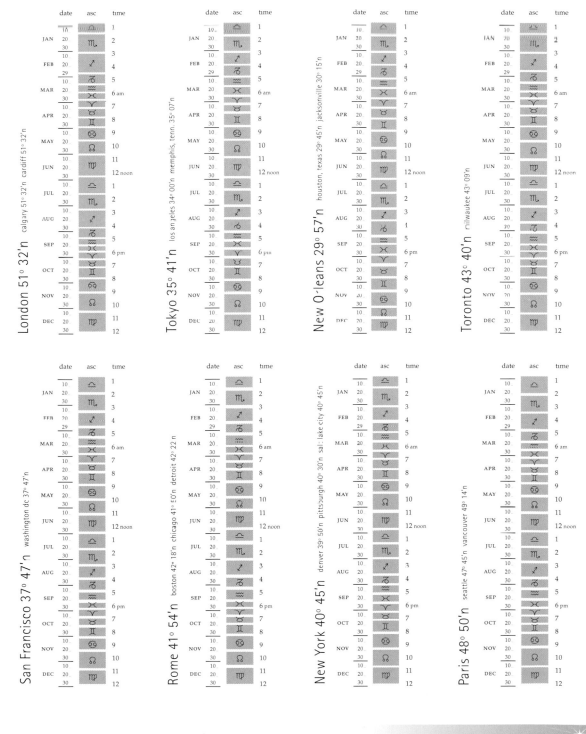

London 51° 32'n (calgary 51° 32'n cardiff 51° 32'n)

date	asc	time
10	♎︎	1
JAN 20	♏︎	2
30		3
FEB 10		
20	♐︎	4
MAR 10	♑︎	5
20	♒︎	
30	♓︎	6 am
APR 10	♈︎	7
20	♉︎	8
30	♊︎	
MAY 10	♋︎	9
20	♌︎	10
30		11
JUN 20	♍︎	12 noon
30		
JUL 10	♎︎	1
30	♏︎	2
AUG 10		3
20	♐︎	4
30	♑︎	5
SEP 20	♒︎ ♓︎	6 pm
30	♈︎	7
OCT 10	♉︎	8
30	♊︎	
NOV 10	♋︎	9
30	♌︎	10
DEC 20	♍︎	11
30		12

Tokyo 35° 41'n (los angeles 34° 00'n memphis, tenn. 35° 07'n)

date	asc	time
10	♎︎	1
JAN 20	♏︎	2
30		3
FEB 20	♐︎	4
29	♑︎	5
MAR 10	♒︎	
20	♓︎	6 am
30		7
APR 10	♉︎	
20	♊︎	8
MAY 10	♋︎	9
20	♌︎	10
30		11
JUN 20	♍︎	12 noon
30		
JUL 10	♎︎	1
30	♏︎	2
AUG 10	♐︎	3
30	♑︎	4
SEP 10	♒︎	5
20	♓︎	
30	♈︎	6 pm
OCT 20	♉︎	7
30	♊︎	8
NOV 10	♋︎	9
20	♌︎	10
DEC 20	♍︎	11
30		12

New O'leans 29° 57'n (houston, texas 29° 45'n jacksonville 30° 15'n)

date	asc	time
10	♎︎	1
JAN 20	♏︎	2
30		3
FEB 20	♐︎	4
29	♑︎	5
MAR 10	♒︎	
20	♓︎	6 am
30	♈︎	7
APR 20	♉︎	
30	♊︎	8
MAY 10	♋︎	9
20	♌︎	10
30		11
JUN 20	♍︎	12 noon
30		
JUL 10	♎︎	1
30	♏︎	2
AUG 10	♐︎	3
30	♑︎	4
SEP 10	♒︎	5
20	♓︎	
30	♈︎	6 pm
OCT 20	♉︎	7
30	♊︎	8
NOV 20	♋︎	9
30	♌︎	10
DEC 20	♍︎	11
30		12

Toronto 43° 40'n (milwaukee 43° 09'n)

date	asc	time
10	♎︎	1
JAN 20	♏︎	2
30		3
FEB 20	♐︎	4
29	♑︎	5
MAR 10	♒︎	
20	♓︎	6 am
30	♈︎	7
APR 20	♉︎	
30	♊︎	8
MAY 10	♋︎	9
20	♌︎	10
30		11
JUN 20	♍︎	12 noon
30		
JUL 10	♎︎	1
30	♏︎	2
AUG 10	♐︎	3
20	♑︎	4
30		5
SEP 20	♓︎	6 pm
30	♈︎	
OCT 10	♉︎	7
30	♊︎	8
NOV 20	♋︎	9
30	♌︎	10
DEC 20	♍︎	11
30		12

San Francisco 37° 47'n (washington dc 37° 47'n)

date	asc	time
10	♎︎	1
JAN 20		2
30	♏︎	3
FEB 20	♐︎	4
29	♑︎	5
MAR 20	♒︎	6 am
30	♓︎	
APR 10	♈︎	7
20	♉︎	
30	♊︎	8
MAY 10	♋︎	9
20	♌︎	10
30	♍︎	11
JUN 10		
20	♍︎	12 noon
30		
JUL 10	♎︎	1
30	♏︎	2
AUG 20	♐︎	3
30	♑︎	4
SEP 20	♓︎	5
30	♈︎	6 pm
OCT 20	♉︎	7
30	♊︎	8
NOV 10	♋︎	9
30	♌︎	10
DEC 10	♍︎	11
30		12

Rome 41° 54'n (boston 42° 18'n chicago 41° 50'n detroit 42° 22'n)

date	asc	time
10	♎︎	1
JAN 20		2
30	♏︎	3
FEB 20	♐︎	4
29	♑︎	5
MAR 20	♒︎	6 am
30	♓︎	
APR 10	♈︎	7
20	♉︎	
30	♊︎	8
MAY 20	♋︎	9
30	♌︎	10
JUN 10		11
20	♍︎	12 noon
30		
JUL 10	♎︎	1
30	♏︎	2
AUG 20	♐︎	3
30	♑︎	4
SEP 20	♒︎	5
30	♓︎	6 pm
OCT 10	♈︎	
20	♉︎	7
30	♊︎	8
NOV 10	♋︎	9
30	♌︎	10
DEC 20	♍︎	11
30		12

New York 40° 45'n (denver 39° 50'n pittsburgh 40° 30'n salt lake city 40° 45'n)

date	asc	time
10	♎︎	1
JAN 20	♏︎	2
30		3
FEB 20	♐︎	4
29	♑︎	5
MAR 20	♒︎	6 am
30	♓︎	
APR 10	♈︎	7
20	♉︎	
30	♊︎	8
MAY 10	♋︎	9
30	♌︎	10
JUN 10		11
20	♍︎	12 noon
30		
JUL 10	♎︎	1
30	♏︎	2
AUG 20	♐︎	3
30	♑︎	4
SEP 20	♒︎	5
30	♓︎	
OCT 10	♈︎	6 pm
20	♉︎	7
30	♊︎	8
NOV 10	♋︎	9
30	♌︎	10
DEC 20	♍︎	11
30		12

Paris 48° 50'n (seattle 47° 45'n vancouver 49° 14'n)

date	asc	time
10	♎︎	1
JAN 20		2
30	♏︎	3
FEB 20	♐︎	4
29	♑︎	5
MAR 20	♒︎	6 am
30	♓︎	
APR 10	♈︎	7
20	♉︎	8
30		
MAY 10	♋︎	9
30	♌︎	10
JUN 10		11
20	♍︎	12 noon
30		
JUL 10	♎︎	1
30	♏︎	2
AUG 20	♐︎	3
30	♑︎	4
SEP 20	♒︎	5
30	♓︎	6 pm
OCT 10	♈︎	
20	♉︎	7
30	♊︎	8
NOV 10	♋︎	9
30	♌︎	10
DEC 20	♍︎	11
30		12

moon tables

Days of the Moon		
Day	Signs	Degrees
1	0	–
2	1	18
3	1	26
4	1–2	39
5	2	52
6	2	65
7	3	78
8	3	91
9	4	104
10	4	117
11	5	130
12	5	143
13	5–6	156
14	6	169
15	6	182
16	7	195
17	7	208
18	8	221
19	8	234
20	9	247
21	9	260
22	10	273
23	10	286
24	10–11	299
25	11	312
26	11	325
27	12	338
28	12	351
29	1	364
30	1	377
31	2	390

	Jan	Feb	Mar	Apr	May	Jun	Jul	Aug	Sep	Oct	Nov	Dec
1928	23°♈	16°♊	10°♋	0°♍	4°♎	18°♏	21°♐	7°♒	26°♓	4°♉	28°♊	6°♌
1929	27°♍	11°♏	18°♏	2°♑	4°♒	20°♓	25°♈	17°♊	11°♌	19°♍	8°♏	12°♐
1930	26°♉	11°♓	24°♓	7°♉	14°♊	8°♌	17°♍	8°♏	25°♐	28°♑	12°♓	14°♈
1931	0°♊	20°♋	28°♋	21°♍	0°♏	21°♐	26°♑	11°♓	25°♈	28°♉	15°♋	22°♌
1932	15°♎	8°♐	2°♑	21°♒	24°♓	8°♉	11°♊	27°♋	17°♍	25°♎	19°♐	27°♑
1933	15°♓	0°♉	8°♉	22°♊	24°♋	10°♍	16°♎	9°♐	2°♒	10°♓	29°♈	2°♊
1934	17°♋	2°♍	10°♍	29°♎	6°♐	0°♒	8°♓	29°♈	16°♊	18°♋	1°♍	3°♎
1935	20°♏	11°♑	19°♑	12°♓	21°♈	12°♊	16°♋	1°♍	16°♎	19°♏	7°♑	14°♒
1936	8°♈	0°♊	24°♊	11°♌	14°♍	28°♎	1°♐	17°♑	8°♓	17°♈	10°♊	17°♋
1937	5°♍	20°♎	28°♎	12°♐	14°♑	1°♓	8°♈	1°♊	24°♋	1°♍	19°♎	23°♏
1938	7°♑	22°♒	1°♓	20°♈	27°♉	21°♋	29°♌	19°♎	5°♐	7°♑	21°♒	23°♓
1939	10°♉	1°♋	10°♋	4°♍	12°♎	2°♐	6°♑	21°♒	6°♈	10°♉	29°♊	7°♌
1940	0°♎	22°♏	15°♐	2°♒	4°♓	18°♈	20°♉	8°♋	29°♌	7°♎	1°♐	7°♑
1941	25°♒	9°♈	17°♈	1°♊	5°♋	23°♌	0°♎	23°♏	16°♑	23°♒	10°♈	13°♉
1942	27°♊	13°♌	21°♌	10°♎	18°♏	12°♑	20°♒	9°♈	25°♉	27°♊	11°♌	13°♍
1943	1°♏	23°♐	2°♑	26°♒	4°♈	23°♉	27°♊	11°♌	26°♍	1°♏	20°♐	29°♑
1944	22°♓	14°♉	6°♊	22°♋	24°♌	8°♎	10°♏	28°♐	19°♒	28°♓	21°♉	28°♊
1945	15°♌	29°♍	7°♎	22°♏	26°♐	14°♒	22°♓	16°♉	8°♋	14°♌	0°♎	3°♏
1946	17°♐	3°♒	11°♒	1°♈	9°♉	3°♋	10°♌	29°♍	15°♏	16°♐	0°♒	3°♓
1947	22°♈	14°♊	24°♊	16°♌	25°♍	14°♏	17°♐	2°♒	17°♓	22°♈	12°♊	21°♋
1948	14°♍	5°♏	26°♏	12°♑	14°♒	28°♓	0°♉	18°♊	10°♌	19°♍	12°♏	18°♐
1949	5°♒	19°♓	28°♓	12°♉	16°♊	6°♌	15°♍	8°♏	29°♐	5°♒	21°♓	23°♈
1950	7°♊	24°♋	1°♌	22°♍	0°♏	24°♐	1°♒	19°♓	4°♉	6°♊	21°♋	24°♌
1951	13°♎	6°♐	17°♐	10°♒	17°♓	4°♉	8°♊	22°♋	7°♍	12°♎	4°♐	12°♑
1952	5°♓	25°♈	16°♉	2°♋	3°♌	17°♍	20°♎	9°♐	1°♒	10°♈	2°♉	8°♊
1953	25°♋	9°♍	18°♍	3°♏	8°♐	26°♑	7°♓	0°♈	21°♊	26°♋	11°♍	13°♎
1954	27°♏	14°♑	21°♑	12°♓	21°♈	15°♊	21°♋	9°♍	24°♎	26°♏	11°♑	15°♒
1955	5°♈	28°♉	9°♊	2°♌	8°♍	25°♎	28°♏	12°♑	28°♒	3°♈	25°♉	3°♋
1956	26°♌	16°♎	7°♏	21°♐	23°♑	7°♓	11°♈	0°♊	23°♋	2°♍	24°♎	29°♏
1957	15°♑	29°♒	8°♓	24°♈	29°♉	20°♋	29°♌	22°♎	12°♐	16°♑	1°♓	2°♈
1958	17°♉	4°♋	12°♋	3°♍	12°♎	5°♐	12°♑	29°♒	14°♈	16°♉	1°♊	7°♌
1959	28°♍	21°♏	2°♐	24°♑	0°♓	15°♈	18°♉	2°♋	18°♌	24°♍	16°♏	24°♐
1960	17°♒	6°♈	26°♈	11°♊	13°♋	27°♌	1°♎	21°♏	15°♑	23°♒	14°♈	20°♉
1961	5°♋	20°♌	28°♌	14°♎	19°♏	11°♑	20°♒	13°♈	3°♊	7°♋	21°♌	22°♍
1962	6°♏	24°♐	3°♑	24°♒	3°♈	28°♉	3°♋	19°♌	4°♎	7°♏	23°♐	28°♑
1963	20°♓	13°♉	24°♉	15°♋	20°♌	5°♎	8°♏	22°♐	8°♒	14°♓	7°♉	15°♊
1964	7°♌	26°♍	16°♎	1°♐	3°♑	18°♒	22°♓	13°♉	6°♋	15°♌	6°♎	11°♏
1965	26°♐	10°♒	18°♒	5°♈	10°♉	3°♋	11°♌	4°♎	23°♏	26°♐	10°♒	12°♓

	Jan	Feb	Mar	Apr	May	Jun	Jul	Aug	Sep	Oct	Nov	Dec
1966	26°♈	14°♊	23°♊	16°♌	25°♍	17°♏	23°♐	10°♒	24°♈	27°♈	14°♊	20°♋
1967	12°♍	6°♏	16°♏	6°♑	11°♒	25°♓	27°♈	11°♊	28°♋	5°♌	27°♎	6°♐
1968	28°♑	16°♓	6°♈	20°♉	23°♊	8°♌	14°♍	5°♏	28°♐	7°♒	27°♓	1°♉
1969	16°♊	0°♌	9°♌	25°♍	1°♏	24°♐	3°♒	25°♓	13°♉	16°♊	0°♌	1°♍
1970	17°♎	5°♐	15°♐	8°♒	17°♓	8°♉	14°♊	0°♌	14°♍	17°♎	5°♐	12°♑
1971	4°♓	27°♈	7°♉	27°♊	1°♌	15°♍	17°♎	1°♐	18°♑	25°♒	18°♈	27°♉
1972	18°♋	5°♍	26°♍	10°♏	13°♐	29°♑	5°♓	28°♈	21°♊	29°♋	18°♍	22°♎
1973	6°♐	20°♑	28°♑	15°♓	22°♈	15°♊	23°♋	15°♍	3°♏	6°♐	19°♑	21°♒
1974	7°♈	27°♉	9°♊	0°♌	9°♍	0°♏	5°♐	20°♑	5°♓	8°♈	26°♉	3°♋
1975	26°♌	19°♎	28°♎	17°♐	21°♑	5°♓	6°♈	21°♉	9°♋	16°♌	9°♎	18°♍
1976	8°♑	25°♒	16°♓	1°♉	3°♊	20°♋	27°♌	20°♎	13°♐	21°♑	9°♈	12°♈
1977	26°♉	10°♋	18°♋	0°♍	12°♎	5°♐	14°♑	6°♓	23°♈	25°♉	9°♋	12°♌
1978	28°♍	18°♏	29°♏	22°♑	1°♓	21°♈	26°♉	18°♋	25°♌	28°♍	17°♏	24°♐
1979	18°♒	10°♈	18°♈	7°♊	10°♋	24°♌	26°♍	11°♏	0°♑	7°♒	1°♈	9°♉
1980	29°♊	16°♌	6°♍	21°♎	24°♏	12°♑	19°♒	12°♈	5°♊	12°♋	29°♌	2°♎
1981	16°♏	0°♑	8°♑	26°♒	3°♈	26°♉	5°♋	26°♌	13°♎	15°♏	29°♐	2°♒
1982	19°♓	10°♉	21°♉	15°♋	23°♌	12°♎	16°♏	1°♐	15°♒	18°♓	8°♉	15°♊
1983	9°♌	1°♎	9°♎	27°♍	0°♑	14°♒	16°♓	2°♉	21°♊	29°♋	23°♍	1°♍
1984	20°♐	6°♒	27°♒	11°♈	15°♉	3°♋	11°♌	4°♎	27°♏	3°♑	20°♒	22°♓
1985	5°♉	20°♊	28°♊	16°♌	24°♍	17°♏	26°♐	16°♒	3°♈	5°♉	19°♊	23°♋
1986	11°♍	3°♏	14°♏	7°♑	15°♒	3°♈	7°♉	21°♊	5°♌	9°♍	28°♎	6°♐
1987	0°♒	21°♓	29°♓	17°♉	20°♊	4°♌	6°♍	22°♏	12°♐	21°♑	15°♓	22°♈
1988	11°♊	26°♋	17°♌	1°♍	5°♏	24°♐	2°♒	26°♓	18°♉	24°♊	10°♌	11°♍
1989	25°♎	10°♐	18°♐	7°♒	15°♓	9°♉	17°♊	7°♌	23°♍	25°♎	10°♐	14°♑
1990	3°♓	25°♈	8°♉	29°♊	6°♌	24°♍	27°♎	10°♐	25°♑	29°♒	19°♈	27°♉
1991	20°♋	11°♍	19°♍	7°♏	10°♐	24°♑	27°♒	14°♈	5°♊	14°♋	7°♍	14°♎
1992	2°♐	17°♑	7°♒	22°♓	28°♈	15°♊	23°♋	17°♍	9°♏	14°♐	29°♑	1°♓
1993	14°♈	0°♊	9°♊	28°♋	7°♍	0°♏	8°♐	27°♑	13°♓	16°♈	0°♊	8°♋
1994	25°♌	18°♎	28°♎	20°♐	27°♑	14°♓	16°♈	0°♊	15°♋	19°♌	9°♎	17°♏
1995	11°♑	2°♓	10°♓	27°♈	0°♊	14°♋	14°♌	5°♎	27°♏	8°♑	29°♒	6°♈
1996	22°♉	7°♋	27°♋	12°♍	16°♎	6°♐	14°♑	8°♓	29°♈	4°♊	19°♋	21°♌
1997	4°♎	20°♏	29°♏	20°♑	29°♒	22°♈	0°♊	18°♋	3°♍	8°♎	21°♏	26°♐
1998	17°♒	10°♈	19°♈	12°♊	18°♋	4°♍	8°♎	20°♏	5°♑	9°♒	0°♈	8°♉
1999	2°♋	22°♌	1°♍	17°♎	20°♏	4°♑	8°♒	27°♓	19°♉	29°♊	21°♌	27°♍
2000	13°♏	27°♐	17°♑	2°♓	29°♓	27°♉	5°♋	29°♌	19°♍	24°♏	8°♑	10°♒
2001	24°♓	11°♉	20°♉	12°♋	21°♌	14°♎	22°♏	8°♑	23°♒	26°♈	11°♊	16°♊
2002	7°♌	1°♎	9°♎	2°♐	7°♑	23°♒	26°♓	9°♉	24°♊	29°♋	21°♍	0°♏
2003	22°♐	12°♒	21°♒	7°♈	10°♉	25°♊	29°♋	19°♍	11°♏	21°♐	12°♒	17°♓
2004	2°♉	17°♊	6°♋	22°♌	26°♍	17°♏	25°♐	19°♒	10°♈	14°♉	28°♊	29°♋
2005	15°♍	6°♏	12°♏	3°♑	14°♒	6°♈	13°♉	29°♊	14°♌	16°♍	1°♏	7°♐

Zodiac signs

♈ Aries
♉ Taurus
♊ Gemini
♋ Cancer
♌ Leo
♍ Virgo
♎ Libra
♏ Scorpio
♐ Sagittarius
♑ Capricorn
♒ Aquarius
♓ Pisces

INDEX

abundance stones 7
Agate 13, 16, 17, 18, 19, 21, 23, 31, 32, 33, 35, 44, 54, 56, 57, 88, 92, 115, 118, 119, 123, 132
alimentary canal 25
Amber 33, 47, 49
Amethyst 13, 36, 37, 51, 53, 54, 55, 82, 83, 107, 112, 130
Amethyst Phantom 124
Ametrine 36, 88, 102, 104, 123
Angel Hair *see* Rutilated Quartz
Angelite 51, 53, 129, 132
Anhydrite 98, 99
ankles 53
Apache Tear 39, 48, 92
Apophyllite 19, 20, 21, 37, 94, 96, 97, 104, 118, 121
Aqua Aura 12, 96
Aquamarine 15, 16, 20, 24, 36, 39, 50, 52, 56, 80, 81, 111, 124, 127, 128
Aquarius
  Ascendant 80–1
  Moon sign 126–9
  Sun sign 50–3
Aragonite 12, 15, 40, 49, 87, 88
Aries
  Ascendant 60–1
  Moon sign 86–9
  Sun sign 10–13
Ascendant 5, 59, 137, 138
Ascendant crystals
  Aquarius 80
  Aries 60
  Cancer 66
  Capricorn 78
  Gemini 64
  Leo 68
  Libra 72
  Pisces 82
  Sagittarius 76
  Scorpio 74
  Taurus 62
  Virgo 70

astrological mandala 6, 135
astrological time 138
Aventurine 11, 86, 88, 97, 103, 130
Azurite 47, 49, 107, 120, 121

back 29, 37
barnacle crystals 32–3
Beryl 24, 41, 54, 56, 92
birthcharts 5, 135–7
birthday rituals 5
  Aquarius 53
  Aries 13
  Cancer 25
  Capricorn 49
  Gemini 21
  Leo 29
  Libra 37
  Pisces 57
  Sagittarius 45
  Scorpio 41
  Taurus 17
  Virgo 33
birthstones 4, 9
  Aquarius 50
  Aries 10
  Cancer 22
  Capricorn 46
  Gemini 18
  Leo 26
  Libra 34
  Pisces 54
  Sagittarius 42
  Scorpio 38
  Taurus 14
  Virgo 30
Black Obsidian 39, 48, 116–17
Black Tourmaline 97
Bloodstone (Heliotrope) 29, 36, 53, 55, 85, 86, 88, 89
Blue Celestite 35, 51, 52, 126
Blue Chalcedony 16
Blue Kyanite 93
Blue Lace Agate 16, 17, 44, 54, 56, 57, 88, 118, 119, 123, 132

Blue Sapphire 34
Blue Selenite 94, 96
Blue Smithsonite 56
Blue Topaz 19, 31, 42, 44, 95, 106, 107, 112
Blue Tourmaline (Indicolite) 70, 71, 92
Boji Stones 17, 53, 62, 63, 129, 132
Botswana Agate 16
bridges 33
Brown Opal 103
Brown Tourmaline 18
buying crystals 6

Calcite 13, 20, 25, 31, 35, 36, 45, 49, 90, 93, 95, 96, 105, 111, 112, 124
Cancer
  Ascendant 66–7
  Moon sign 98–101
  Sun sign 22–5
Capricorn
  Ascendant 78–9
  Moon sign 122–5
  Sun sign 46–9
Carnelian 25, 29, 36, 89, 95, 99, 103, 104, 109
Cathedral Quartz 29, 49
Cat's Eye 26
Celestite 31, 35, 51, 52, 111, 126, 131, 132
Cerussite 87, 113, 119, 127
Chalcedony 16, 19, 23, 25, 98, 127
challenges
  Aquarius 51–2
  Aries 11
  Cancer 23
  Capricorn 47
  Gemini 19
  Leo 27
  Libra 35–6
  Pisces 55
  Sagittarius 43–4
  Scorpio 39–40
  Taurus 15
  Virgo 31

Charoite 39, 43–4, 45, 107, 116, 119, 124, 127
Cherry Opal 113
Chiastolite 35, 128, 132
Chrysanthemum Stone 20, 124
Chrysoberyl 88, 108, 110
Chrysocolla 19, 21, 24, 99, 103
Chrysoprase 24, 41, 52, 88, 99, 129, 131
circulatory system 29, 53
Citrine 11, 13, 36, 68, 69, 100, 103, 108
cleansing crystals 7
Clear Quartz 13, 126
crystal balls 129
crystals 4, 6, 7, 9
Cymophane 131

Danburite 133
Dendritic Agate 33, 35
Dendritic Chalcedony 19, 23
Diamond 10, 116
Dioptase 39, 45, 100, 103, 117

elimination system 41
Emerald 14, 119
emotions
  Aquarius 52, 127–8
  Aries 12, 87–8
  Cancer 23–4, 99–100
  Capricorn 48, 123–4
  Gemini 19, 95–6
  Leo 27–8, 104
  Libra 36, 111–12
  Pisces 56, 131–2
  Sagittarius 44, 119–20
  Scorpio 40, 115
  Taurus 15–16, 91–2
  Virgo 32, 108
endocrine system 37
energy 9

feet 57
Fire Agate 13, 23, 115, 132
Fire Opal 37

Fluorite 35, 47, 48, 49, 51, 52, 131
Fuchsite 53, 55, 104, 109, 133

Galena 48, 125
Garnet 28, 29, 40, 43, 46, 47, 48, 78, 79, 109, 119, 122, 127
Gemini
  Ascendant 64–5
  Moon sign 94–7
  Sun sign 18–21
gemstones 6, 7
glyphs 9
Golden (Imperial) Topaz 20, 29, 39, 104
Green Agate 92, 115
Green Calcite 13, 90, 93, 124
Green Chlorite Phantom 124
Green Jasper 116
Green Kunzite see Hiddenite
Green Sapphire 34
Green Tourmaline 16

Hawk's Eye 39, 40, 88, 114, 117
healing 7
  Aquarius 53
  Aries 13
  Cancer 25
  Capricorn 49
  Gemini 20–1
  Leo 29
  Libra 37
  Pisces 57
  Sagittarius 45
  Scorpio 41
  Taurus 17
  Virgo 33
heart 29
Heliotrope see Bloodstone
Herkimer Diamond 116
Hiddenite (Green Kunzite) 21, 27, 39, 102, 108
hips 45
Howlite 11, 19, 20, 21, 100

Imperial Topaz see Golden Topaz

Indicolite see Blue Tourmaline
insomnia 21, 53
intestines 33
intuition 85
Iolite 112
Iron Pyrite 11, 87, 123

Jade 99, 112
Jadeite 49
Jasper 11, 24, 35, 52, 60, 61, 89, 99, 100, 108, 116, 119, 132
Jupiter 77, 83

kidneys 37
knees 49
Kunzite 12, 13, 27, 28, 36, 87, 93, 104, 131
Kyanite 56, 64, 65, 90, 93, 96, 108

Labradorite 43, 44, 45, 47, 51, 115
Lapis Lazuli 15, 17, 35, 119, 120
Larimar 39, 103, 111, 113
Lavender-Pink Smithsonite 115
Lavender-Violet Smithsonite 32
Leo
  Ascendant 68–9
  Moon sign 102–5
  Sun sign 26–9
Lepidolite 57, 92, 119
Libra
  Ascendant 72–3
  Moon sign 110–13
  Sun sign 34–7
liver 45
lunar crystals 85
lymphatic system 57

Magnesite 33, 57, 87, 123
Magnetite 51, 91
Mahogany Obsidian 35
Malachite 15, 16, 38, 40, 41, 44, 91, 117
Mangano Calcite 35, 36, 111
Mars 11, 61, 75

masks 59
  Aquarius 80, 81
  Aries 60, 61
  Cancer 66, 67
  Capricorn 78, 79
  Gemini 64, 65
  Leo 68, 69
  Libra 72, 73
  Pisces 82, 83
  Sagittarius 76, 77
  Scorpio 74, 75
  Taurus 62, 63
  Virgo 70, 71
meditations
  Aquarius Ascendant 81
  Aries Ascendant 61
  Cancer Ascendant 67
  Capricorn Ascendant 79
  Gemini Ascendant 65
  Leo Ascendant 69
  Libra Ascendant 73
  Moon signs 85
  Pisces Ascendant 83
  Sagittarius Ascendant 77
  Scorpio Ascendant 75
  Taurus Ascendant 63
  Virgo Ascendant 71
Mercury 31, 65, 71
Moldavite 51, 127
Mookaite 92
Mookaite Jasper 61
Moon 5, 22, 67, 85
Moon crystals
  Aquarius 126
  Aries 86
  Cancer 98
  Capricorn 122
  Gemini 94
  Leo 102
  Libra 110
  Pisces 130
  Sagittarius 118
  Scorpio 114
  Taurus 90
  Virgo 106
Moon signs 137, 138
Moonstone 22, 23, 25, 51, 52, 53, 55, 56, 57, 66, 67, 98, 99, 100, 123
Morganite (Pink Beryl) 28, 55, 99, 100, 105, 131
Moss Agate 21, 31, 32, 33, 115, 119

Nebula Stone 32, 121
needs
  Aquarius 127
  Aries 87
  Cancer 99
  Capricorn 123
  Gemini 95
  Leo 103
  Libra 111
  Pisces 131
  Sagittarius 119
  Scorpio 115
  Taurus 91
  Virgo 107
Neptune 83
nervous system 33

Obsidian 35, 39, 40, 48, 96, 116–17
Okenite 106, 108, 120
Onyx 46, 48
Opal 24, 34–5, 36, 37, 100, 103, 113
Opal Aura Quartz 132
opaque stones 6
Orange Calcite 31

past lives
  Aquarius 129
  Aries 89
  Cancer 100–1
  Capricorn 125
  Gemini 97
  Leo 105
  Libra 113
  Pisces 132–3
  Sagittarius 120–1
  Scorpio 116–17
  Taurus 93
  Virgo 109
Peach Aventurine 88
Peridot 15, 16, 30, 31, 90, 91, 92, 107, 109
personality types 9
Petalite 24, 100–1
Phantom Quartz 124
Pietersite 47, 57, 106, 109, 124
pineal gland 53
Pink Beryl see Morganite
Pink Carnelian 36, 95, 103
Pink Chalcedony 25, 98
Pink Tourmaline 12, 23, 99

Pisces
  Ascendant 82–3
  Moon sign 130–3
  Sun sign 54–7
pituitary gland 57
planets 59
Pluto 38, 75
potential
  Aquarius 50–1
  Aries 11
  Cancer 23
  Capricorn 46–7
  Gemini 19
  Leo 27
  Libra 35
  Pisces 54–5
  Sagittarius 43
  Scorpio 39
  Taurus 15
  Virgo 31
Prehnite 91
psychosomatic disease 33
Purple Fluorite 35, 49, 52
Pyrolusite 125

Quartz 13, 17, 20, 27, 29,
  39, 40, 41, 44, 45, 49, 52,
  57, 72, 73, 74, 75, 86, 89,
  90, 91, 105, 108, 110, 114,
  115, 117, 122, 124, 126,
  128, 132

Red Aventurine 88
Red Calcite 45
Red Garnet 29, 40
Red Jade 88
Red Spinel 45
Red Tourmaline 31, 44
reproductive system 25, 41
respiratory system 21
Rhodochrosite 27, 28, 29,
  40, 52, 95, 96, 103, 105,
  113, 117, 124, 131
Rhodonite 15–16, 24, 25,
  91, 92, 99, 117, 121, 127
Rhomboid Calcite 96
Rhyolite 45, 120
Rising sign see Ascendant
rituals 5
  attracting love 113
  birthday see birthday
    rituals
  co-operation 89

forgiveness 117
grail 121
inner voice 125
letting go 93
opening the heart 105
releasing vows 109
scrying 129
tie cutting 56, 101
truth 97
unconditional love 133
Rose Quartz 27, 52, 72, 73,
  105, 110, 128
Royal Sapphire 97
Ruby 10, 23, 24, 28, 29, 45,
  47, 87
Ruby in Zoisite 131
Rutilated Quartz (Angel
  Hair) 17, 20, 90, 91, 114

Sagittarius
  Ascendant 76–7
  Moon sign 118–21
  Sun sign 42–5
Sapphire 32, 34, 95, 97
Sardonyx 30, 32, 107, 111
Saturn 52, 79, 81, 128
Sceptre Quartz 41, 117
Scorpio
  Ascendant 74–5
  Moon sign 114–17
  Sun sign 38–41
scrying 129
Selenite 15, 56, 57, 92, 94,
  96, 99, 127, 133
Serpentine 19, 125
shins 53
skeletal system 49
skin 49
Smithsonite 32, 56, 115
Smoky Phantom 124
Smoky Quartz 13, 39, 40,
  45, 57, 74, 75, 108, 114,
  115
Snow Quartz 44, 86, 89,
  122, 124
Snowflake Obsidian 40, 96
Sodalite 48, 56, 99, 120
soul pathway
  Aquarius 53
  Aries 12
  Cancer 24
  Capricorn 48
  Gemini 20

Leo 28–9
Libra 37
Pisces 57
Sagittarius 45
Scorpio 41
Taurus 17
Virgo 32–3
soulmate crystals 37, 127
Spinel 45, 109
Staurolite 107
Stibnite 49
stomach 25
stress 13, 20, 50
substitutes, gemstones 6, 7
Sugilite 32, 33, 35, 45, 52,
  97, 110
Sulphur 128
Sun 26, 69
Sun signs 5, 9, 59, 137
Sunstone 24, 87, 100, 101,
  124, 131

Taurus
  Ascendant 62–3
  Moon sign 90–3
  Sun sign 14–17
thinking
  Aquarius 52
  Aries 12
  Cancer 24
  Capricorn 48
  Gemini 20
  Leo 28
  Libra 36
  Pisces 56
  Sagittarius 44
  Scorpio 40
  Taurus 16
  Virgo 32

throat 17
Thulite 41
thymus gland 21
thyroid 17
Tiger Iron 60
Tiger's Eye 26, 27, 28, 35,
  104, 108, 132
Topaz 16, 19, 20, 27, 28, 29,
  31, 39, 40, 41, 42, 43, 44,
  76, 77, 95, 102, 104, 106,
  107, 112, 118, 120
Tourmaline 11, 12, 16, 18,
  23, 28, 31, 44, 94, 97, 99,
  112
tumbled stones 6
Turquoise 38, 42–3, 44, 55,
  117

Ulexite 35
Uranus 52, 81, 128

Vanadinite 32, 128
Variscite 19, 97
Venus 14, 63, 73
Violet Spinel 109
Virgo
  Ascendant 70–1
  Moon sign 106–9
  Sun sign 30–3

Watermelon Tourmaline 11,
  28, 112
Wulfenite 35, 112, 113, 119

Yellow Calcite 105
Yellow Sapphire 32

zodiac 9

ACKNOWLEDGEMENTS

Photography: **Octopus Publishing Group Limited/**
Mike Hemsley/Andy Komorowski/Guy Ryecart

Executive Editor Brenda Rosen
Managing Editor Clare Churly
Executive Art Editor Sally Bond
Designer Colin Goody
Picture Librarian Jennifer Veall
Production Controller Aileen O'Reilly